YOUR
MOVE

YOUR MOVE

WHAT **BOARD GAMES** TEACH US ABOUT LIFE

JOAN MORIARITY & JONATHAN KAY

sh.
SUTHERLAND
HOUSE

TORONTO, 2019

Sutherland House
416 Moore Ave., Suite 205
Toronto, ON M4G 1C9

Sutherland House and logo are registered trademarks of The Sutherland House Inc.

First edition, September 2019

If you are interested in inviting one of our authors to a live event or media appearance, please contact publicity@sutherlandhousebooks.com and visit our website at sutherlandhousebooks.com for more information about our authors and their schedules.

Manufactured in Canada
Cover designed by Greg Tabor
Book composed by Karl Hunt
Game photos by Sean Jacquemain, Photographer and Managing Editor of dailyworkerplacement.com

Endpaper photos from *The Checkered Game of Life* (front) and the modern edition of *The Game of Life* (back).

Library and Archives Canada Cataloguing in Publication
Title: Your move : what board games teach us about life /
Joan Moriarity, Jonathan Kay.
Names: Moriarity, Joan, author. | Kay, Jonathan, 1968- author.
Description: Includes index.
Identifiers: Canadiana 20190106018 | ISBN 9781999439545 (softcover)
Subjects: LCSH: Board games. | LCSH: Board games—Social aspects.
Classification: LCC GV1312 .M67 2019 | DDC 794—dc23

ISBN 978-1-9994395-4-5

CONTENTS

CHAPTER ONE

Welcome to the Magic Circle

(Joan Moriarity: Lessons from Telestrations*)*

WORK AT Snakes & Lattes Board Game Café in Toronto. My official job title is Game Guru. Guests sometimes tell me that I must have the best job in the world and usually I find it hard to disagree. It is certainly the most rewarding work I have been paid to do and my experiences have led me to co-write this book.

Board games have undergone a tremendous resurgence in the past twenty years but even today I occasionally meet people who are surprised to hear that anyone still plays games on a tabletop instead of some kind of electronic device. (In this book, we'll use the terms "board game" and "tabletop game" interchangeably, even when the games in question do not involve an actual board). In hindsight, perhaps it was inevitable that people would welcome the chance to turn away from their screens, seeking the warmth and connection you get from playing games together with live human family and friends.

Despite its popularity, this hobby can be tricky for newcomers. If you heard somewhere that tabletop games are "back" and you want to see what all the excitement is about, you come up against two big problems right away: you need to decide which game to play, and you need to learn the rules. My work has taught me that either of those problems can end a beginner's journey before it starts. Most of the new people who walk into Snakes & Lattes end up defaulting to the old chestnuts of their youth—*Guess Who?, Snakes and Ladders, Connect Four*—instead of striking out into this bright new world of games to try something they have never seen before. That is unless they have someone to guide them. That is where I come in.

Every day at work, I help people to find games that will suit their tastes and I help them learn to play so that they do not need to struggle through a rule book. I began doing this shortly after Snakes & Lattes opened in 2010 as North America's first board game café. Dozens of similar places have since opened in other cities and what began as a board game renaissance has matured into a new golden age.

There has never been a better time to play games with your friends around a table because there has never been such an extraordinary variety of great games to play. You could stick to the games of past centuries, if you like. You could also stick with the music or movies or literature of previous centuries but that would mean missing out on a lot of amazing things. And if you do so while I am on the job—if you insist on limiting yourself to games from fifty years ago, even if it is for a good reason—I cannot help feeling that I have failed you as a game guru.

My co-author, Jonathan Kay, is a prime example of someone who has jumped in with both feet and embraced everything this reinvigorated artistic medium has to offer. He and I come at the project from different directions: while I am a lifelong game junkie who has become a writer in recent years, he is a lifelong writer who has become an avid game player over the last decade. While I love to introduce games to others and enjoy the hobby's deep and nuanced social dimensions, Jonathan tends to be more focused on games' historical and cultural overtones. While Jonathan tends to focus more on lessons about society at large, I tend to examine how playing games can teach us about an individual human soul.

The difference is probably easiest to spot when it comes to the one title that takes center stage in not one but two chapters of this book: *Monopoly.* My own chapter on *Monopoly* examines the reasons why so many people today still enjoy a game from 1935 even though, to the eyes of modern game players, it has aged poorly. Jonathan, on the other hand, focuses on the manner in which *Monopoly*'s internal structure models the functioning of our economy, our climate, and our history of warfare. That said, both of us came to this project with one thing in common: we see the playing of games not only as a fun way to spend time but as a window into the human condition.

This is not a book of strategy tips or game reviews. It is about the things games can teach us about ourselves. Each chapter focuses on one or two game titles (though references to other games will be scattered about), and draws out a revealed lesson in history, psychology, philosophy, society or culture. Each chapter is designed to stand as an individual essay, so you do not have to read the whole thing in order from start to finish.

* * *

I have already mentioned two big gateway issues that new players face: deciding what to play, and coming to grips with rules. But there is a third problem, one that is, perhaps, more serious than the others: fear of failure. Not a simple issue, as any therapist can attest, but it is something that games have a lot to teach us about if we allow them to. I will approach it here by doing what I do best: I am going to teach you how to play a game.

The best game I can think of to teach you, and illustrate this third problem, is *Telestrations* (2009). It is a cross between *Pictionary* and the broken telephone game. You can play with as few as four players, but it is better with more. Each player gets a little spiral-bound booklet full of blank plastic pages, a dry-erase marker, and a secret word or phrase. To begin, you open your booklet to page one and draw a picture of your secret word. You'll need to work fast because you only have about one minute to get it done. And if you think that doesn't sound like enough time to do a good job of it, you are absolutely correct.

When time is up, you pass your booklet clockwise to the player sitting on your left, while the player to your right passes you their booklet. Now you look at the (probably terrible) picture on page one of the booklet you have just received and try (and probably fail) to figure out what it is supposed to be. Then you flip to page two and write down your guess, and pass clockwise to your left again. The player on your right passes you a booklet open to page two with a guess of some kind written there, and now you have one minute to draw a picture of *that* on page three. And so on. Sketch and pass, guess and pass, sketch and pass, guess and pass.

Once your little booklet has gone all the way around the table and come back to you again, it's time for show-and-tell. You announce your secret word and hold up your sketch from page one for all to see. Then you turn to page two and show everyone what the person on your left thought you had drawn. Turn to page three and show everyone the next player's picture of that guess, and then to page four to show what the next player thought *that* was, and so on.

Usually, by the time it gets back around to you, neither the words nor the pictures have anything whatsoever to do with your original word. And just like in the broken telephone game, that's the point. The game is rigged to make everyone fail as hilariously as possible.

Telestrations is silly even before you get to the reveal. The panic that sets in when you realize you are almost out of time generates nervous laughter and sitting around a table full of laughing people makes it hard not to start laughing along with them. Reading the other players' bizarre guesses before trying to figure out some possible way of capturing those guesses within the limits of the time frame (as well as the limits of your own artistic capabilities) is also giggle-inducing.

But the biggest laughs always come at the end during show-and-tell. Seeing how your initial word or phrase wound up garbled beyond recognition, including the bad drawings people made and the weird guesses they came up with based on those bad drawings—if you have any ability to laugh at yourself, it's hard not to.

As fun as *Telestrations* can be, it is not guaranteed to entertain, however. Even among players who want to enjoy it, and are willing to laugh at themselves, there are two ways the game can go wrong. The first is too much success. If the clues are too easy (or all the players are skilled speed sketchers), the game is hardly worth playing. You might start with the word "cheese" and draw a nice little sketch of a piece of cheese, then pass it on to the next player, who correctly identifies it as cheese and passes it on to the next player, who also draws an easily identifiable piece of cheese, and so on. By the time it gets back around to you, nothing has changed. Everyone has succeeded. Which is boring. Some clever *Telestrations* players have even instituted a house rule to the effect that if you are good at drawing, you have to use your off-hand. It is a rule I heartily endorse.

The second way the game can go wrong is too little effort. A player who simply is not interested in the game might draw some random scribbles, which are not really meant to look like anything at all. Or they might lazily guess something totally unrelated to the sketch they have been given. Either way, it is not entertaining for them, or for anyone else at the table. Desperate incompetence is funny, and in this context, endearing. Apathetic indifference? That's just ruining everyone's fun.

For *Telestrations* to deliver on its premise, the players need to do two things. First, they must try their sincere best to succeed and, second, they must fail. Because that is the fun of it—the joyous, flailing panic as you realize how bad you are at this, and the gentle *schadenfreude* of laughing at your friends' equally silly struggles.

Although I am only talking about one particular game, I believe this truth applies to nearly every game. If you are an absolute perfectionist, there is no room for fun. Likewise, if you are too bored or lazy to even bother trying, it spoils the game for the whole table. To enjoy play, to be playful, the freedom to fail is as essential as the will to succeed.

* * *

Here is a conundrum though. If this kind of playful approach is so important, why is it completely absent from all the games that seem to matter on a cultural level today? Think about it. What are the games that get talked about in mainstream media coverage? They tend to come in three categories: professional sports, high-stakes poker, and reality TV shows.

Notice the common factor? Players in these games are not allowed to be playful. They are not allowed to mess up. If you make a mistake in any of those spheres, you will not have a good time like you would in *Telestrations* or any of the other games I tend to recommend at the café. You know right from the outset that failure will result in severe real-world consequences. You could lose your career or your bankroll. You could be humiliated in the eyes of millions of people.

When people think of games, they aren't thinking of *Telestrations*. They're not thinking about something that is fun for everyone, win or lose. The image in their mind is of a kind of gladiatorial battle with life-and-death stakes, with every slip-up broadcast for all the world to see.

It was not always like this. Old-fashioned board games used to be something that just about anyone could (and did) play and enjoy. And rest assured, games today are much better than they have ever been. Their design, components, production, artwork, ease of play, depth—everything about them has advanced over the decades. So why are we so afraid to play?

* * *

Nobody needs to be told that it is important to try your best to succeed. And the freedom to fail is also an essential element of being creative, as we learned from watching all those TED Talks. "You'll never come up with anything original if you're not prepared to be wrong," says Sir Kenneth Robinson. And that is true. "It's better to try and fail than not to try at all," the motivational poster tells us. And it would be nice to be able to live our lives that way, would it not?

But we don't. And there is a simple reason for that. We know all too well what will actually happen if we try and fail. The motivational poster says one thing but our lives at school and at work have taught us exactly the opposite lesson: stay in your lane, follow procedure, do not stick your neck out, and do not screw up. If you take an unconventional approach to a school project, you risk a failing grade. At work, a bold initiative that costs your company money may cost you your job, even if the idea was promising. If at a dance club, wedding, or bar mitzvah reception, you try some moves that require a little more skill than you possess, you might become an unwilling viral YouTube sensation.

The brutal reality of our lives has taught us that when we face a challenge, there are only two acceptable outcomes. Succeed brilliantly on your first attempt, or do not try at all: the very same two things guaranteed to ruin the fun of *Telestrations*, or most any other game. And we have learned these lessons well. We ignore the slogans that tell us to be daring and obey the unspoken rules that tell us to be invisible, even though we well know that the challenges of our time will not be solved without bold, creative approaches. We have gotten so good at discouraging creativity and playfulness that we are terrified to try anything else. These fears run so deep that they even invade the one realm that should always be safe from such considerations—our playtime. I know this because I see it every time I go to work.

Like the librarian who rarely has time to read, I do not get the chance to play games nearly as often as I would like. But I do get to enjoy them vicariously through the people I help, when they are willing to let me help them—which happens less often than you might imagine because all too often they are afraid that someone might see them fail. At playing. They worry that they will not understand the rules of a new game, or that they will make dumb moves, and that their friends (who may well be struggling with the very same fears) will then think they are stupid.

Every night at work, I watch people as they approach that big wall of board games we keep at the back of the café. It does not take a mind reader to tell how intimidated they feel. Sometimes, they are tired from a long week of work and they just want to relax. Sometimes, they have had a few beers and are not in shape for anything too demanding. Sometimes they just happen to have a personal preference for simple, uncomplicated experiences. But often I hear them chuckle awkwardly on being asked if they would like some help, or see them freeze on being invited to try an unfamiliar game, and then reflexively reach for the comfort and safety of *Snakes and Ladders* or *Battleship*. They might not admit it, even to themselves, but I know what fear looks like. All too often, the main reason they avoid new games is that they see them not as a chance to be playful but as a minefield of public shame and disgrace.

I will go into this later on when I talk about *Monopoly* but for now, suffice to say that over the years I have learned to understand a good many legitimate reasons why some people gravitate toward games more appealing for their associated nostalgia than their substance. And I get the sense that my co-author makes peace with that same fact, in his own way, in his chapter on *Scrabble* (which he does not seem to like any better than I do *Monopoly*). But even though I get why people do it, I cannot help feeling sad every time I see someone recoiling at the thought of trying something different. Everything you love was new to you at one point, and if you had not taken a chance and tried it that first time, you would not be enjoying it today.

Games, at their best, have the power to create a special space, a world within the world. It's a kind of magic circle where different rules apply. Inside the magic circle, failure is not only accepted but welcomed. Even necessary. As everyone who has ever played *Telestrations* knows, failing in a game is not the same thing as failing in real life. In real life, failure can be an unparalleled teacher and a stepping stone to success. But in play? *Failure is the whole damned point.* Failing does not mean you are bad at being playful. If you are failing and still enjoying yourself, that means you are doing it right. It means the magic circle is protecting you, just as it is supposed to do.

* * *

There are plenty of factors that can cause that magic circle to fail, though, and we'll be covering many of them in the chapters ahead. Our sensitivities and biases, our fears and recriminations, our past experience and future expectations can all conspire to make even a casual game feel as deadly serious as a job interview after months of desperate unemployment. Much depends on context. Every time you start a new game, you and your fellow gamers make unspoken decisions about how much of the real world will be allowed to come inside the circle. On one side of the spectrum are, say, professional poker players and other high-stakes gamblers for whom the magic circle is non-existent. The game is literally their life. On the other side of the spectrum are fantasy gamers who meet up at tournaments or gaming conferences to construct collectively elaborate in-game universes, sometimes without ever even learning each other's real-life names. The entire universe they share lies within the magic circle. And when the game ends that universe implodes. Most gamers lie somewhere in between these two extremes with their position on the spectrum being a function of their personality.

That includes my co-author and I. Jonathan is a journalist and former engineer who loves to tease out the patterns that link the abstract world of gaming with real life, even when it comes to controversial subjects. And so he treats the game world more as an intellectual laboratory than an emotional sanctuary and enjoys passing from one side of the circle to the other. By contrast, my own essays reflect a more protective attitude towards the integrity of the magic circle. I have spent much of my career at Snakes & Lattes amidst many personality types, observing all the different ways in which their enjoyment and, indeed, their sense of self-worth can be threatened when the circle is compromised. Making sure everyone at the table has a good time is not only my job but my duty.

Another difference in approach lies in our research methodology. As a teacher at a board game café, my "research subjects" arrive at my doorstep every day unbidden (and pay my employer for the privilege). Jonathan, on the other hand, has adopted a more conventional shoe-leather approach, interviewing board game designers, visiting gaming tournaments in North America and Europe, reading essays by gaming fans and critics, and playing lots and lots of board games.

As the book rolls on, the chapters get longer, and the games become more complex. While our early material tends to focus on party games such as *Telestrations* and nostalgia-soaked titles such as *Life* and *Monopoly*, later chapters explore games with heavier themes: zombies, racism, ethnic warfare. In these chapters, Jonathan and I will wrestle with some assumptions we first brought to the writing process. In "Discovering Myself—by Invading Belgium," his final chapter, Jonathan turns his gaze inward, explaining how, more than four decades into his life, he finally came to understand the way his brain works following an epic seven-hour war-gaming session at a youth hostel in Copenhagen.

I also use chapters later in the book to confront my own biases and limitations as a gamer (and game teacher). After having spent years observing people playing a popular but intellectually down-market title called *Cards Against Humanity*, I thought I had a clear sense of that game as an outlet for casual bigotry. And I felt confident in my thoroughly uncharitable assessment of the people who played and enjoyed such games. But, as readers will see in the chapter entitled "Horrible People," the reality is that I had much more to learn about what makes a game welcoming or unwelcoming to players, and I still do.

I have made it my life's purpose to help people rediscover how it feels to be playful, to rehabilitate the value of play and diminish the stigma and fear of failure, to help game players experience the joy of an uncertain outcome, and the exhilaration that comes from throwing yourself into the unknown. I hope that as you read this book, you will enjoy looking at games through my eyes and through Jonathan's. I hope you will find your own reasons to embrace play and make it a part of your life, through both new games and old favorites.

And if, like almost everyone I meet at work, your insides squirm a little at the thought of being judged for your failure to be good at playing, you might consider making *Telestrations* your first step into the magic circle. Perhaps more than any other title in this book, it is the game that will welcome you and help you to experience this ancient and magical truth: laughter destroys fear.

CHAPTER TWO

Peaceful Games From War-Torn Europe

(Jonathan Kay: Lessons from
The Settlers of Catan, Power Grid)

THE MODERN BOARD GAME renaissance is an economic development that would have been hard enough to imagine a generation ago when video games were taking over living rooms. It seems even more improbable today, given that each of us carries a miniature video arcade around inside our smartphone. As of 2018, the data showed that U.S. board game sales grew by 28 percent between the spring of 2016 and the spring of 2017, with revenues expected to rise at a similar rate into the early 2020s—largely, reported one analyst, because the target audience "has changed from children to adults," particularly younger adults.

Much of this success is traceable to the rise of games that get those adults acting more like children. As my co-author will be explaining later in this book, clever, low-overhead card games such as *Cards Against Humanity*, *Secret Hitler*, and *Exploding Kittens* ("A card game for people who are into kittens and explosions") have become standout performers. And thanks to Kickstarter, anyone with a great idea and a contact at an industrial printing company can circumvent the usual toy-and-retail gatekeepers who green-light new concepts. As of this writing, the largest project category on Kickstarter is "Games," with board games making up about three-quarters of the listed projects.

Another area of swift growth has been the category of "hobby" board games, which comprises more sophisticated titles oriented toward serious adult players—think *The Settlers of Catan* (or, as it has been known since 2015, just *Catan*). These more complex games once represented a niche segment, but that is starting to change: according to *ICv2*, a trade publication that covers board games, comic books, and other hobbyist products, sales of hobby board games in the United States and Canada increased from an estimated $75 million to $305 million between 2013 and 2016, the latest year for which data was provided.

At the 2017 and 2018 iterations of Gen Con in Indianapolis— North America's largest hobby-gaming convention—turnstile attendance topped sixty thousand (up from about thirty thousand in the early 2000s). And attendance might have been even higher if the venue (Lucas Oil Stadium) had been more accommodating. And in 2017, for the first time in event history, all attendee badges were purchased before the event began.

Inspect a graph of Gen Con attendance since its founding in 1968 by *Dungeons & Dragons* co-creator Gary Gygax and you will find a small but steady uptick throughout the 1970s and 1980s when annual attendance reached about ten thousand, followed by a sudden, rapid increase in the 1990s. The short explanation for this phenomenon is that the gaming industry started producing better games that more people wanted to play. Understanding how it did so, however, requires that we examine the innovations embraced by leading late twentieth-century designers. By way of case study, I can think of no better specimen than Phil Eklund, whose professional trajectory perfectly tracks the creative explosion in board gaming over the last four decades.

Eklund, born and raised in the United States, took to game design early in life. As a teenager in Tucson in the 1970s, he became frustrated with the narrow, child-oriented "roll-and-move" titles on offer at local toy stores. He started creating his own games, making photocopied print runs of a few hundred and mailing them out to customers. Within America's then-tiny board game subculture, Eklund was making a name for himself. But he felt like part of the lowest caste of nerds. "I'd go to a gaming convention, and everyone would be crowded around the computers," he told me in a 2018 phone interview. "My board game setup would be off in the corner. The only people who'd wander over were the folks looking for a garbage can so they could throw out their gum."

That is in the past. Eklund now lives in Germany, where he has attained the status of cult celebrity in the Eurogaming world. He has no plans to move back to the United States. "One of the reasons I came to this country is because I knew it was the place where people take board games really seriously," he told me. "The designers have status. They put their name on the box, and people will buy based on their reputation."

Eklund's friends now include such board game masterminds as Friedemann Friese, the creator of *Power Grid*, and the legendary Uwe Rosenberg, who has designed award-winning Euro-classics such as *Agricola*, *Le Havre*, and *Patchwork*. At Germany's world-leading *Internationale Spieltage* (International Game Day) fair in Essen—which now attracts an audience from all over the world numbering almost two hundred thousand (several times the attendance at Gen Con)—these bookish introverts are mobbed by groupies seeking selfies. "It's not like I destroy hotel rooms or go out with movie stars," Eklund tells me. "But it's sufficiently intense that when I get back home, it takes a week just to recover."

Hobbyists outside of Europe started paying serious attention to German-style board games (or Eurogames, as they are now more commonly known) following the publication of *The Settlers of Catan* in 1995; and once these games started to edge out the old "Ameritrash" (as older American-style board games are derisively called), there was no going back. Much in the way that Cold War–era American beer connoisseurs gravitated to the higher quality and substantially larger variety offered by European imports in the era before stateside microbrews took off, sophisticated hobbyists who had become bored with the usual rec-room fare started to dedicate themselves to the inventive new titles coming out of Europe.

Catan has many of the signature features associated with Eurogames: randomized board layouts, flexible scoring systems offering multiple paths to victory, and an aesthetic that tends toward rustic themes and wooden pieces. There is something much deeper going on here, too. As Eklund and other Eurogame pioneers have explained to me, the philosophy of play embedded within the game is rooted in long-term historical trends dating to World War II.

In North America, the complex board games created during the latter half of the twentieth century typically took the form of simulated warfare. In *Risk*, *Axis & Allies*, *Star Fleet Battles* and *Victory in the Pacific,* players take on the role of generals moving their units around tabletop maps. For obvious reasons, this was not a model that resonated positively with Germans who grew up in the shadow of the Third Reich. Which helps explain why all the most popular Eurogames are based around building things instead of destroying them—communities (*Catan*), civilizations (*Terra Mystica*), farms (*Agricola*), rail networks (*Ticket to Ride*). The result is a vastly more pacifistic style of a game that can appeal to women as much as men, and to older adults as much as high-testosterone adolescents.

"When I was young, one of my first creations was a *Star Trek*-type game with humans fighting other races in space," Eklund says.

"I now realize it was more or less a racist concept. It's been done many times. It's just not that interesting." In Germany, by contrast, he has created games such as *Pax Renaissance*, in which players take on the role of bankers navigating the vicissitudes of war and religious upheaval in upheaval in fifteenth- and sixteenth-century Europe; and *Greenland* (which gets its own chapter later in this volume), in which players compete for walrus tusks and whale blubber as ancient hunters and sailors.

The gulf between Ameritrash and Eurogames goes beyond the divide between militarism and pacifism. *Monopoly*, that great bonfire of friendships, is not a wargame. Nevertheless, the conflict among players is direct, brutal, and zero-sum: you bankrupt me or I bankrupt you. Which is why so many rounds of *Monopoly* finish on a note of bitterness. (The one game of *Monopoly* I ever played with my wife ended with her staring me down icily and declaring, without any hint of warmth or irony, "I have never seen this side of your personality.")

In Eurogames, by contrast, bare-knuckled competition is outré. The Spanish-themed *El Grande*, for instance, does not permit players to attack their opponents directly. Rather, players maneuver their caballeros around a map of medieval Spain in a bid to win the favor of local courtiers. Much as in *Catan*, players do not beat their opponents so much as out-grow them. The same is typically true in rail-themed Eurogames such as *Ticket To Ride*, in which players rush to claim choice routes between cities. The action is always *passive* aggressive, never full-on aggressive.

Moreover, once the thematic requirement of combat was removed from the equation, Eurogame designers realized that they could incorporate virtually any theme into high-level strategy gaming. One of my current favorites, for instance, is a little game called *Biblios*, in which each player takes on the role of an abbot seeking to amass the greatest possible library of sacred books. The aforementioned

Uwe Rosenberg has created bestselling games on the theme of quilting (*Patchwork*, 2014), harbor development (*Nusfjord*, 2017) and Bavarian glass-making (*Glass Road*, 2013).

The scoring systems for Eurogames tend to reward the amassing of different kinds of resources—not just money. And there is an enormous amount of fussy micro-managerial satisfaction to be had in earning wood and brick so you can build a road, which allows you to build a settlement, which gets you stone so you can build a city which in turn pumps out more wood. This churn of multi-colored cards and tokens can make Eurogames seem overly complicated to outsiders. And they do tend to have a lot of different phases and checklists—in Friedemann Friese's masterpiece *Power Grid*, there is even a step called the "bureaucracy" phase.) But in practice, all the busywork keeps players immersed in their own projects, and less spiteful towards others' success. Which makes for gentler competition, fewer arguments and (in my experience) less in the way of marital recrimination.

Since the Eurogame genre formally came into being roughly four decades ago (the inception of Germany's Spiel des Jahres award, celebrating the "game of the year," would peg 1978 as a rough start of momentum-gathering), the earliest creators understood something fundamental about the psychology of gaming. While players can tolerate losing at evening's end, they despise the feeling of being eliminated from a game in progress. To be forced from the table while your friends are still having fun can feel a little too much like grade-school social rejection.

And so almost every Eurogame is designed so that final scoring comes only at the end of the game, after some defined milestone or turn limit so that every player can enjoy the experience of being a (nominal) contender until the final moments. If this sounds somewhat Euro-socialistic, that is because it is (as will be discussed in more detail in my chapter dedicated to *Monopoly*, later in the book).

But such mechanisms acknowledge the real-life social reality that no one wants to block off three hours for gaming only to get knocked out early and bide their time watching TV as everyone else continues to have fun.

Perhaps no game encompasses this gentle Eurogaming ethos more fully than the aforementioned *Power Grid* (or *Funkenschlag*, as it is known in Germany), in which players take on the role of CEOs in a highly regulated, centrally administered energy market. While the first player who builds houses and hotels in *Monopoly* can leverage her initial advantage to build yet more houses and hotels and crush the competition, the opposite dynamic is at work in *Power Grid*. The more players expand their energy networks, the lower their priority in acquiring the coal, oil, uranium and recyclables they need to fuel their power plants. The feature acts as a natural damping mechanism on runaway leaders, so that players tend toward parity as the action progresses and almost every game is fairly close until the last turn.

This way of playing caters to what most people actually want out of game nights, and post-World War II life more generally: to unwind and compete, to remain friends, and to live out one's days in bustling little towns and harbors, as opposed to battle-ravaged hellscapes lorded over by warring generals.

CHAPTER THREE

A Checkered Life

(Joan Moriarity: Lessons from The Game of Life*)*

L IFE ISN'T WHAT IT used to be, and neither is *The Game of Life*.

Milton Bradley's life was filled with painful lessons about the cruelty of chance. In the early nineteenth century, Bradley's father invested what little fortune the family had on a new process to extract starch from potatoes, just before America's potato crops were wiped out by the same plague that caused the Great Famine in Ireland. While the family moved from one New England town to the next in search of better work, young Milton studied hard and was eventually able to start a lithography business, achieving success with a popular portrait of Abraham Lincoln the year he was elected. Shortly afterwards, Honest Abe decided to grow a beard, making Bradley's entire inventory worthless. He was ruined.

His deeply held belief in the virtues of hard work and perseverance were nevertheless unshaken, and he was rewarded for it, appropriately enough, through a game he created to teach the virtues of hard work and perseverance. With its straightforward rules, simple yet meaningful decisions, and strong moral overtones, *The Checkered Game of Life* (1860) was an immediate hit.

There had been plenty of other track-based games before, descendants of *Snakes & Ladders* in which you would roll a die, move a piece, and obey the instructions on the space where you landed. *The New Game of Human Life*, published more than half a century earlier in 1790, was one such game, and it was dreadful. That precursor had adopted the determinism of *Snakes & Ladders* and actually made it worse by incorporating puritanical "life lessons." For example, if you land on The Romance Writer at the fortieth space on the board, you are sent back to The Mischievous Boy at five. But if you land on The Tragic Author at forty-five, you proceed directly to The Immortal Man on the final eighty-fourth space and win immediately. Unintentionally hilarious for today's audiences, perhaps, but still not much fun to play.

The life lessons in Milton Bradley's *The Checkered Game of Life* were no less didactic yet Bradley introduced something important to the equation: choice. For how could sin exist in a world without free will?

Here is how you played. Dice were considered morally suspect at the time (being associated with gambling dens) so instead of rolling a die you spun a teetotum (a six-sided spinning top that produces exactly the same effect as a die without all those unpleasant associations). And rather than being forced to obey the result, you were presented with a choice. On a result of one, you were allowed to move one space and you could choose to move up or down. On a two, you could go one space left or right, and on a three you could go one space in any diagonal direction. Fours, fives and sixes were better versions of (respectively) ones, twos or threes, offering identical choices of direction but with the added option of moving two spaces instead of one, if desired.

When you landed on a space, you might be instructed to move to a different space ("INTEMPERANCE: go to POVERTY"), or you may have earned points toward your eventual victory ("HONOR:

Five points"). The first player to score one hundred points would win the game. These points were meant to represent not only achievement, money, and fame, but also the spiritual rewards of a life well led. The most profitable space by far is "Happy Old Age" at the top right corner of the board, which would score you a massive fifty points.

Because of the way the board was laid out with its rewards and punishments, you might at times have been left with no choice but to go to a punishment space, perhaps because you were on the edge of the board with only one direction to go, or perhaps because you spun a one and the spaces directly above and below you were both undesirable. But you got yourself into that mess by your own free choice. You entered that space between GAMBLING and IDLENESS knowing it was a risk, knowing that the teetotum might send you to prosperity and victory, or leave you with two options, both of them bad. You could play it safe in *The Checkered Game of Life*, or you could take chances, or you could do a bit of both. Each approach had its advantages and its drawbacks. And although luck played a strong role, you could live the kind of life you chose to live, if you were willing to accept the consequences.

The Checkered Game of Life saved Bradley's business, which eventually grew to become one of the biggest game publishers in the world. In 1960, to commemorate the company's centennial, a new version of *The Game of Life* was devised and published. It was to be a true re-imagining, a game to bring Milton Bradley's original vision of life into the modern era. This is the game you may remember from your childhood rec room, and which may still have a place in your attic. When you see it on the tabletop next to a picture of the 1860 original, a hundred years' worth of advances in manufacturing and production are immediately apparent. The simple checkerboard with its tiny illustrations has been replaced by a sprawling plastic landscape of roads, hills, bridges, and buildings.

The dice-free tradition has been kept but instead of offering a flimsy teetotum, *The Game of Life* provides a brightly colored spinner built into its rolling hills. And to go with all this luxury, more luxury: millions of dollars in paper money, stock certificates, promissory notes, and insurance policies. Little plastic cars with little holes in which to place your little pink and blue plastic spouse and children. The beautiful, modernist box simply overflows with *stuff.*

The Game of Life also scored a prestigious celebrity endorsement from television personality Art Linkletter, whose famous TV broadcasts of the opening of Disneyland turned the then-unproven concept of a "theme park" into an enduring cultural phenomenon. With all this going in its favor, the new edition of *The Game of Life* became such a smash hit that its wildly successful predecessor is all but forgotten today.

Presentation and production values were not the only elements that had changed, however. Despite everything that was added, one very important aspect was dropped: choice. Every time you play *The Game of Life*, you will get a car. You will get a house. You will get a job, and you will get a spouse (of the opposite gender, of course). And this is just at the get-go. As play continues, you will spin the spinner, move your car as instructed, then read and obey the instructions on the space where you land. You will have children when the game instructs you to have children. You will follow the path laid out for you. What few choices you can make come down to simple probability analysis. If the expected value of buying insurance is greater than the required investment, the correct move is to buy it. And why would you ever not make the correct move? It was a return to 1790 and the *Snakes & Ladders* style determinism of the pre-Milton Bradley *New Game Of Human Life,* with a colorful 1960s face-lift and a whole lot of needless, pretty complexity.

Another big change lay in the game's moral stance. Those pre-twentieth-century, track-based games tended to share one thing in common: your goal would be to lead a virtuous life. This, too, was abandoned by game designers in the postwar period in favor of material wealth. Players no longer scored points to measure the health of their soul. Instead, they collected money, and at the end of the game, the richest player was declared the winner.

In later decades, minor changes were introduced, including random bonuses or penalties for doing things considered moral or immoral at the time ("Open a health food chain! $20,000"). In the end, however, it was always money that determined your victory or defeat. Mammon had conquered *Life*.

The board game collection at Snakes & Lattes gets used a lot, so the popular games wear out quickly. We have gone through more than a dozen copies of *The Game of Life*. And for the most part, they have been played to death by people in their twenties and thirties, not children. You might think that demographic would prefer modern games such as *Catan* to throwbacks such as *Life*. It is not always so.

Traditionalists have criticized more recent editions of *Life* for various reasons, including the addition of career and salary cards, the removal of fire insurance and changes in content to reflect contemporary ideas of virtuous behavior ("Build a dolphin sanctuary! $50,000"). But watching the café clientele playing all these different versions, only one change seems to have really made a difference to them: the removal of the 3-D plastic hills and bridges in the 2014 edition. While players might grumble a bit about changes in content, they tolerate them. Take away the scenery though, and their level of interest falls off a cliff.

And this brings us full circle. The original *Checkered Game Of Life* was meant to edify players so that they would live virtuous lives. The form of the original game was little more than a checkerboard with a few illustrations and a cardboard spinner. It sold itself on the basis of its content. The appeal of the twentieth-century re-imagining of *Life,* by contrast, has been its idyllic toy landscape. Harsh but fair life lessons have been replaced by a nostalgic *Leave It To Beaver* fantasy world in which everyone gets a job, everyone gets a house, and everyone finds their lifelong soulmate, right at the beginning of their journey through adult life. And, unlike *Monopoly,* everyone gets rich—it is only a question of how rich.

Yes, the winner is determined arbitrarily by random chance. What of it? So what if your success or failure is almost completely outside your control? Is there anyone under the age of forty today who believes the real world is any different? It's a stupid, unfair game, and everyone knows it. But spend a little time watching millennials playing *The Game of Life* at a game café and you may notice something: they do not always feel compelled to play by the rules.

If a gay man is playing, you can bet he will have two blue pegs in the front of his little plastic car (assuming he has not rejected traditional gender color assignments altogether). Some players might decide it does not make sense that you do not get to pick your career, and they will just choose the one they like, randomness be damned. A few might even decide there is no good reason they should not be able to buy and sell one another's children. The free-form exploration of "playing house" replaces the strictures of the rule book (which was never much fun to read anyway), and all that remains of the 1960 original is its adorable setting and silly Boomer-era preconceptions, which are just as easy to subvert as they are to accept.

Although ignoring or inventing new rules for a game is not a recent phenomenon, and it is certainly not unique to *Life,* perhaps it has special meaning for a generation raised largely without hope for a better world or prospects for anything like a "Happy Old Age." The Victorians and the boomers were mostly content to play by the rules, secure in their faith that virtue would eventually find its reward, if not in this game (or in this world) then in the next. But some from the younger generation appear to have decided that when a game is boring or unfair, maybe it does not make sense to play by the rules. When life (or *Life*) is not what it should be, maybe it is time to change the game.

CHAPTER FOUR

An Offer You Can't Refuse

(Jonathan Kay: Lessons from Chinatown *and* No Thanks!*)*

F OR GAMERS WHO LOVE the art of the deal but do not want to waste precious gaming time rolling dice and pushing tokens around a *Monopoly* board, *Chinatown* is the perfect choice. In this real estate game, created in the late 1990s by German designer Karsten Hartwig, properties are distributed to players randomly at the beginning of every turn. The bulk of the game consists of pure negotiation.

While the properties in *Monopoly* are named after streets in Atlantic City, *Chinatown* takes its inspiration from the early days of New York City's original Chinese commercial area near Canal Street. The *Chinatown* playing surface looks something like a giant chessboard, and each player (the fun is maximized with five people) use assigned chessboard squares to erect little cardboard flower shops, restaurants, tea houses, laundromats, and other street-level retail businesses.

The drive to deal with other players is embedded in the scoring rules which emphasize economies of scale. Tiny businesses that cover only one or two board squares do not earn a lot of points (even when calculated on a per-square basis), while big bonuses are awarded for expanded businesses that sprawl over four, five, or six contiguous squares. Players typically start the game with scattered, isolated properties, then consolidate their holdings into big, connected blocs in order to maximize scoring.

The opening layout of a player's properties typically dictates her deal flow. For instance, if I have a growing tea house in one sector of the map, and you own a single, unused square that is adjacent to my tea business, it will make sense for you to sell me that single rump square so that I can build more tea-house seating and score big points, assuming I am willing to pay you a decent price.

Or we may *trade* properties. Instead of me paying you money for your unused, isolated square, I might offer you another rump square that I own in another area of the map, close to your main hub—which may, for instance, allow you to add more washers and dryers to a growing laundromat. There is always going to be a market-clearing price (one that meets supply and demand) for this kind of transaction, because orphaned squares always generate a lot more revenue once they are tacked on to an existing business.

In this way, *Chinatown* is a sort of extended case study in the purest form of microeconomic decision-making. All players are out to maximize their own profits, and the costs and benefits are transparent. The game shows how, in this kind of perfect world, capitalism can make everyone richer.

That exchange of properties described in the paragraphs above, for instance, might be analogized to the real-world case of two collectors who each own incomplete sets of fancy dishware. If Collector A has seven place settings of Wedgwood China in a *Charnwood* pattern, and one setting in *Florentine Turquoise*; while Collector B has seven place settings of *Florentine Turquoise* and one of *Charnwood*, then it makes both collectors better off if Collector B gives up the rump

Charnwood setting in exchange for Collector A's rump *Florentine Turquoise*, thereby generating two complete sets of eight (which are, as any collector knows, apt to fetch a much higher price than incomplete sets of seven). Indeed, if these collectors were not somehow able to reach terms on such a mutually profitable deal, one might conclude that at least one of them was irrational.

And yet, human nature being what it is, this sort of irrational actor does sometimes pop up. I know this to be true because sometimes that irrational actor is me.

* * *

As I recall, it was late 2016, and I was playing a five-player game of *Chinatown* with some neighborhood friends, including an avid gamer by the name of John Chew (whose name will pop up again later in the book). The game was unfolding in the typical *Chinatown* way, and the lay of the land clearly suggested that John and I would soon be making a deal. In one corner of the board, John had an antiques shop that he could expand if he acquired my neighboring rump property, while elsewhere on the board, I had a florist that could be expanded to its full capacity if John sold me his two adjoining unused squares. The deal looked promising and fair for both of us. While John would be giving me two squares, and I would be giving him only one, his fully built-out antiques shop would generate roughly double the revenue of my completed florist.

But then John did something startling. He started an entirely *new* business on one of the two squares that I coveted, an irreversible move (the game rules do not permit businesses to be removed once they are placed on the board) that massively lowered my expected value in any prospective deal. To revert to the dishware example described above, it was as if John had taken a teacup I coveted, and permanently repurposed it as a cheap desk ornament.

John calmly assured me that the deal still was a good idea for both of us. Yes, it was true, John acknowledged, that he would now be giving me much less than I had originally wanted. But since I would still be making *some* extra revenue on the deal, and since John was the only player who had any interest in buying my rump property, the deal still should make sense for me. Put another way, he had me over a barrel. In economic terms, he was operating within a monopsony, a market in which there is effectively only one buyer. With no one else buying what I had to sell, my best play was to swallow my pride and sell out to John, even though he had deliberately tanked the price I would be receiving.

In purely microeconomic terms, John's argument was flawless. And I quite clearly remember thinking that accepting this diminished deal was the rational thing to do. Yet as I began handing over the property token, my muscles seized. Something in me rebelled against the situation. It grated on me that John would be benefiting from behavior that I regarded as opportunistic and cynical. So I balked.

At this point I should point out that, to my knowledge, I am generally known among other gamers as a reasonably good sport. I like to win. I am competitive and sometimes mope around a bit if on a losing streak. But I never yell or throw an out-and-out hissy fit when things do not go my way. So my peevish decision to reject John's deal was out of character. What's worse, it arguably put me outside the "magic circle" that my co-author Joan described eloquently in the introductory chapter, as it blurred the line between real-life personal pride and in-game strategizing. As a gamer, I pride myself on being a dispassionate analyst who knows how to play the odds. What was it about this situation that made me abandon the cut-and-dry tools of cost-benefit analysis?

The implications of this question go beyond the world of games. Microeconomics is built around rational choice theory, which presumes that economic actors will consistently act in such a way as to maximize the value they receive in any transaction. But at that gaming moment, Rational Choice Theory left the building, even when John specifically appealed to its precepts. "Forget it, John," I told him. "It's *Chinatown*." (I did not actually say this but wish I did.)

* * *

Since the early 1980s, social scientists have talked about the Ultimatum Game. It is not really a game in the sense of *Chinatown* or the other games described in this book. Rather, it is a game in the sense of game theory, an academic field that applies mathematical models to describe and test the way people make real-life decisions.

The Ultimatum Game involves two strangers, one of whom is designated as "the proposer," and the other as "the responder." The researcher conducting the Ultimatum Game will offer the proposer a gift (e.g., one hundred dollars in cash) that must be shared with the responder. The proposer then decides how to split up the gift, and informs the responder of the proposed division of spoils. If the responder accepts the split, then both participants receive their assigned portion. But if the responder rejects the split, neither player receives anything. In either case, the proposer and responder never learn one another's identity.

In a purely rational world, it would not matter how the proposer divided the gift. So long as the receiver gets *something* out of the deal, she should always accept what is offered—even if it is as lopsided as ninety-nine dollars for the proposer, and one dollar for the receiver. (After all, a single dollar is better than nothing.) But what researchers consistently find is that responders often will reject proposed splits that are significantly lopsided. Most responders are okay with splitting the money 60/40, and possibly even 70/30. But once the ratio becomes higher than that, responders often balk. What is more, proposers seem to *anticipate* this "irrational" behavior among responders, as studies show that the average proposed split in Ultimatum Game trials is about 60/40.

Ultimatum Game experiments conducted around the world show that this sort of behavior is exhibited universally among men, women, poor, rich, young and old. It also transcends cultural differences. When one set of researchers conducted the Ultimatum Game in Jerusalem, Ljubljana, Pittsburgh and Tokyo, for instance, it got roughly similar results.

So what explains the irrational-seeming impulses of Ultimatum Game participants? There are many theories, but several clues emerge from follow-up experiments in which researchers tinkered with the rules. In the 1990s, for instance, Gary Bolton and Rami Zwick created the Impunity Game. In this variation of the Ultimatum Game, the responder retains the right to accept or reject the proposed division of spoils. This decision does not affect the proposer, who always will retain the amount that she originally apportioned to herself. For example, if a proposer offers a responder just ten dollars out of a hundred dollar sum, then the proposer would keep her ninety dollar portion, regardless of whether the responder agreed to accept her ten dollar portion.

The results were stark. Unlike in the Ultimatum Game, responders in the Impunity Game were willing to accept even the most meagre payout. Bolton and Zwick had hypothesized that Ultimatum Game responders might be rejecting small payouts because accepting them might serve to diminish their dignity in front of the researchers conducting the experiment. But results from the Impunity Game suggest that Ultimatum Game responders who leave money on the table are motivated primarily by a desire to punish a proposer's "unfair" offer—a reflex that some might classify as spite.

The question then becomes this: why are humans so eager to punish anonymous individuals for their perceived greed? Even if the proposer in an Ultimatum Game truly does learn a life lesson about equity and social justice from a responder's decision to punish him for a lowball offer, how does that benefit the responder? (Remember, in these games, the participants are strangers to one another.)

The answer would seem to be rooted in evolutionary psychology. While most of us now live in cities full of strangers, our primate brains emerged in an ancestral environment where we existed almost exclusively in small, tight-knit kin groups. Even as recently as a few centuries ago, most European peasants lived their whole lives in farming communities populated by just a few dozen families. In such environments, where everyone knows everyone, community members tend to deal harshly with behavior deemed disruptive or anti-social to help ensure that it does not happen again. Even today, the idea of punishment and retribution comes naturally to us and explains how mobs are so easily stirred to acts of vengeance following a shocking crime.

At the same time, none of us want to be viewed by our peers as a sucker who can be easily be exploited by others, the economic equivalent of cuckoldry. Imagine a peasant farmer who is offered pennies on the pound for her crops. One can understand why she might prefer to let that produce rot in the fields rather than give in to an unscrupulous, bargain-hunting buyer. The farmer concludes, not unreasonably, that it is economically worse, in the long term, to gain a reputation as an easy mark than to squander a small one-time payment. As my own experience shows, such instincts are so indelibly marked on our brains that they flare up even when we are playing a game with no real-world consequences, easily blasting through the intellectual conceit of the "magic circle" that supposedly protects in-game Jonathan from the anxieties and hubris of real-life Jonathan.

In the Ultimatum Game, every game is a one-off event. In real life, which is what has conditioned our brains over the millennia, we tend to deal with the same colleagues, friends and family members day in and day out. It is this reality that has programmed our evolutionarily engineered decision-making circuitry. By punishing proposers who offer unfair deals, we are exhibiting behavior that, while irrational with regard to a one-off transaction with a stranger, may be rational as a long-run strategy to show onlookers that you will not let them enrich themselves by targeting you with predatory commercial behavior.

Consider an analogy from the criminal sphere. Who are you going to rob: the victim who will just shrug his shoulders because he knows that it is more rational to hand over his wallet than risk his life, or the hothead who will "stupidly" fight to the death as a matter of principle and honor? Who is the more feared baseball pitcher: the high-precision control artist who puts the ball on the corner of the strike zone every time, or the wild man whose fastballs are just as likely to come straight at your head? In the sterile context of the Ultimatum Game, spite and unpredictability are interpreted as indicators of irrational behavior. In real life, they can help intimidate competitors and discourage predators.

In that 2016 game of *Chinatown*, it was not just John who was observing me. It was three other players. What message would it have sent if I had taken that deal? True, I wound up losing *this* game of *Chinatown* by rejecting a strategy of pure profit maximization. But by showing everyone that I was willing to "punish" hardball deal-making with mutually destructive behavior, I was paving the way for improved fortunes in the future.

* * *

There is another way that the Ultimatum Game can be unrealistic. It focuses exclusively on bilateral relations between one proposer and one responder, whereas real life often involves a multitude of actors, and thus far more unpredictability. One way to understand how this unpredictability affects the decision-making of economic agents is through a simple little game of cards and tokens called *No Thanks!* In some ways, it can be like the Ultimatum Game. In my experience, however, the mechanics are more psychologically complex—and illuminating.

No Thanks! is popular because the games are short, the rules are easy, and there are a lot of (often hilarious) taunts and acts of brinksmanship. Also, you can play in large groups of five, six or even seven players. The 2004 brainchild of German designer Thorsten Gimmler, *No Thanks!* is played with a deck of thirty-three cards numbered, in order, from three to thirty-five. Before each new game is played, the deck is shuffled, and nine of the cards are randomly removed from play, face down. The remaining deck of twenty-four cards is then placed face down in the middle of the table. One by one, each card is turned face up and auctioned off, until all twenty-four cards are claimed, and the game is over.

The auctions in *No Thanks!* are unusual because in the early part of the game, at least, no one actually wants the cards. Each card is worth the printed number of points (the 8 card is worth eight points, and so forth). And as in golf, high scores are bad. So a player who ends the game with, say, the 10 card, the 12 card, and the 18 card (for a sum of forty points), will beat a player who has the 15 card and the 30 card (for a sum of forty-five points). The fewer the points you have, the better.

All auctions require some form of currency. In *No Thanks!*, this currency consists of circular red tokens, each of which has a point value of negative one (remember: low scores are *good*—so the tokens are valuable), with each player receiving eleven tokens at the beginning of each game. As you might imagine, it is good to end the game with few cards and lots of tokens. In some cases, a winning player who scores an especially spectacular victory, with lots of tokens in her possession, may finish the game with a negative score.

For each of the twenty-four cards auctioned, the procedure is as follows: the starting player has the option of either taking the auctioned card into her possession *or* she may say "no thanks," place one of her tokens on the card, and pass the card (and any chips that she and others have placed on it) clockwise to the next player, who then must choose between the same two options. In some cases, cards will make the clockwise circuit of the table repeatedly. Each player will say "no thanks" and add a chip to the pile on the card, until the number of chips becomes so great that a player decides it is worth his while to take the card, chips and all. That player then becomes the starting player for the next auction.

If that is all there were to the game, the decision-making arithmetic in *No Thanks!* would be childishly simple. Do not take a card of value X unless there are at least X chips on it. But the rules provide an interesting twist. When a player's hand includes a *continuous* run of cards, say, 18, 19, 20, 21, and 22, it is only the lowest-numbered card of that run that counts for scoring. So a hand that consisted solely of the cards 18, 19, 20, 21, and 22 would score as just eighteen points, instead of one hundred points (the sum of all five cards).

Thus, as the game progresses, different cards will take on different values to different players. If I already have the 18 card in my possession, the 19 card is "free" for me if I take it because it will not add any points to my hand. It will be very costly for any other player who takes it (assuming that player does not have the 20 card). And if the 19 card comes to me with a few tokens from other players who already have passed on it, so much the better. Taking the card will reduce my score.

Except that even if a card is "free" for me, or allows me to make a profit, I might not take it *just yet*. I may instead let it go clockwise around the table one more time (or even more than once), so that all of my adversaries can pile yet more tokens on the card, allowing me to reap an even bigger bonanza by the time the card circles the table and gets to me again.

In my gaming group, this tactic always causes grumbling. "You're milking the cow!" people will say to the player everyone knows will eventually take the card. Or there will be mock accusations of price gouging. Even though players know that there is nothing personal going on, that the cow-milking player is merely doing the rational thing to maximize her chance of winning, resentment inevitably builds as the pile of tokens sitting on the card gets large. "Oh, just take it!" other players will say with semi-mock exasperation. No one likes to feel he is over a barrel, even in a game.

Of course, a player who holds the 18 card would only let a chip-laden 19 card escape her grasp if she thought that none of the other players would take it. And this is where the skill of the game comes in. As with the Ultimatum Game, knowing what your own profit-maximizing move will be in any given situation requires you to predict the behavior of others. Except that instead of predicting the behavior of one person, you have to predict the behavior of several. How close are they from achieving emotional escape velocity from *their own* magic circles? All it takes is one person to grab the card you covet, and your winning strategy can be thwarted.

Which brings me to the classic *No Thanks!* situation I once found myself in with the aforementioned John Chew and his two sons (who also happen to be skilled and enthusiastic gamers). It was a game in which the deck was down to the very last card, which happened to also be the highest card: 35. This suited me quite nicely since I happened to possess the 34 card in my hand.

All my opponents groaned when this final card was revealed, and with good reason. They all knew that this would be a 35-point poison pill in their own hands but a free (or better) card in mine. When an udder is this fat, I figured, you have to milk it for a good long time. I expected to be sending the card around the table two, three, maybe four times, watching the pot of chips grow until I finally claimed the card and the many tokens that would come with it. In the meantime, I reaped a windfall of *schadenfreude*: with every chip, my opponents were forced to add to the pot, their groans grew more piteous. Then came grumbles and muttered recriminations. All in good fun, of course. Kind of.

By this point in a *No Thanks!* game, the arithmetic is truly stark because there are no longer any unknowns. The last card has been exposed. I knew that on the level of rational play I could keep sending that 35 card around the table until it had thirty-five chips. Anything less than that number and it simply made no sense for anyone except me to grab it.

But before the jackpot could build, something happened that filled me with doubt. "One of us should just take the card to make Jon angry!" said Liam, John's youngest son. He laughed and so did others. Me too, nervously. As I stared at the card, I thought, "Would Liam really do that?" Would he sabotage his own score and take on the spoiler role as a booby prize? Surely, not.

But if not Liam, would someone else do it? Indeed, maybe Liam's outburst had been aimed at intentionally planting the idea in the minds of others. He was only in Grade Five at the time yet in my experience he was no stranger to mind games. I looked around the table at my four opponents. Did I feel comfortable predicting what John would do? Maybe. What Liam would do? Perhaps. What everyone would do? No.

I looked down at the 35 card in front of me. There were a dozen chips on it. Send it around again and I would get a bunch more. Then more after that. With each progressive iteration, I knew, the sense of spite would grow more acute among my competitors. Moreover, the cheers—I knew there would be *actual cheers*—would grow louder for the player who came forward to thwart me. All it takes is one hothead to get fed up and grab the pot. "I may be going down," I imagined this as-yet-unknown nemesis saying to me, "but I'm taking you with me!"

It struck me at that moment that this is not just the logic of *No Thanks!* and the Ultimatum game but also of social justice, of Marx, of Robin Hood, of revolution. Throughout history, has it not been this same pattern that has driven peasants and campus radicals alike to reckless gestures of violent protest as a means to strike fear into the hearts of upper classes? When the rich take a dozen chips, the sansculottes will grumble. Keep bleating *let them eat cake* as you feast on their tokens and eventually, they will storm the palace. For each protestor who is cut down by the bayonets or thrown into prison, the cost of revolution surely exceeds the benefits. For the mob as a whole, well, that might be a different story.

I took those twelve chips and ended the game. In doing so, I grimly noted the irony of the outcome. It had not been Liam or anyone else who had acted "irrationally." It was me, acting out of fear that *they* might act irrationally.

Such are the complexities of real-life decision-making. Which is why economists, for all their formulae and data, will never fully succeed in modeling the way we all think.

CHAPTER FIVE

Cures for Pandemics and Alpha Players

(Joan Moriarity: Lessons from Pandemic)

BUSINESS CONSULTANTS and corporate human-resources people spend a lot of their time helping executives manage conflict, which inevitably occurs when team members have incompatible goals. Sometimes, however, the reasons for flagging morale in an organization are not incompatible goals but disagreement on how best to achieve an agreed-upon goal.

Here is an example. A team of lawyers has been tasked with a complex legal problem. The team is composed of several senior partners and a few juniors. At first, everyone is happy and united. As time passes, pressure builds, and the file becomes more complicated, and the seniors get frustrated by the slow pace and high error rate of the juniors. Eventually, they start doing all the work themselves, relegating the juniors to mundane clerical roles. The job gets done. No one yells at anyone, or even says a harsh word. It does not seem like there is any real conflict here. Yet everybody ends up frustrated, especially the juniors, who are left wondering why they were brought on to the project in the first place.

Scenarios like this, which probably arise more often in most companies than episodes of outright hostility, are hard to manage because they are not covered by standard mechanisms for resolving disputes, like rules of workplace conduct. The only way to address them is through some kind of unspoken company-specific *meta-rules* about the trade-offs that are and are not acceptable between short-term goals such as task efficiency and long-term goals such as mentorship, morale, and staff retention.

Believe it or not, this is a common problem faced by board game designers, and some have come up with novel solutions for addressing it. I am not exaggerating when I say that certain kinds of board games can help your organization solve—or at least identify—conflicts that arise when different people within the organization have different assumptions about the best way to balance short-term task execution with long-term capacity development.

But before we get into that, let's start with some basics. Allow me to introduce you to the concept of *the play contract.*

Whenever you sit down to play a game, whether you realize it or not, you are entering into an unspoken agreement with your fellow players. There is no universally agreed-upon text for the play contract. But if there were, it might include these basic precepts, which flow from our discussion of the magic circle in the book's first chapter:

1. I agree to abide by the rules of the game as I understand them; no cheating.
2. I agree to take the game seriously enough to make a sincere effort to win; no throwing the game.
3. I agree to not take the game so seriously that it will affect my real-life relationships with my fellow players; no behaving like a jackass.

The problem is that the second and third points sometimes come into conflict. How hard do you have to play to satisfy the need for a sincere effort? How easy do you have to take it on your fellow players to keep things from getting too heavy? Those stories you have heard about wounded feelings and damaged friendships: in many cases, they are caused by players coming to the tabletop with conflicting answers to these questions.

It is worth exploring exactly why that second point of the play contract is so important. Why shouldn't we just pull a structurally integral block out of the *Jenga* tower and collapse it at the start of the game? Why shouldn't we move our king out into the middle of the chessboard? Why shouldn't a *Monopoly* player offer to accept rent payment in the form of pop tarts?

Sometimes, in some games, the answer is "no reason." If you are playing a very casual game, antics like these might be entertaining and fun for everyone. And as long as everyone at the table understands the play contract as such, you can enjoy the silliness and have a grand old time. (In the next chapter, we will also get into the way a game's narrative can take on greater importance than its victory conditions, leading to situations where you do not try to win because that is not how the story should go. But that is not typically the case.) If someone brings out a board game to play, that someone is looking to engage with you through the structure of that game as it was intended to be played, not to perform improv comedy (unless that is actually part of the game), and they do not want to attempt random stunts. They want to try to overcome a challenge. Maybe they want that competition to be relatively loose and friendly, or maybe they want it to be more serious. Either way, if you start clowning around and deliberately making moves that make no sense, your fellow players will become annoyed. You are not playing the game as they see it and that is a violation of the play contract which they thought everyone tacitly agreed to at the start of the game.

Even a serious-minded player can cut loose and have fun playing dumb sometimes, and even a party animal can hunker down with something brainy and challenging when she feels like it. But if you want a game to be fun for everyone playing, they all need to be in it together. Games are most enjoyable when everyone at the table gets to have a good time, and that is what the play contract is there for: to make sure everyone has a good time. When everyone is invested enough in a game to feel excitement and tension, wondering how it will turn out, but detached enough to not feel like a failure as a human being if they lose, that is the sweet spot where all the best play happens.

Preserving that tension and keeping the game's outcome uncertain is tricky. If the game is going to be any good, that tension needs to be there. As soon as everyone realizes what a game's outcome is going to be, the game is, for all intents and purposes, over. That is why game enthusiasts get so annoyed when someone at the table breaks with the second precept of the play contract and does not make a reasonable effort to play his best. If you are not trying, we know you are not going to win. No uncertainty, no game.

Here's an analogy from the world of humanity's best friends. If you are a dog owner, ask yourself how your dog signals that she wants to play. If she is like most other dogs, she starts out with a gesture that may be described as "mock adversarial." If you start putting on a sock, she will grab it with her teeth and start pulling it off, hoping for some kind of tug-of-war. Or, if you are in your backyard together and you approach her, she will get down into a bowing position, wag her tail and scamper off diagonally left or right while maintaining eye contact with you. What she is saying is, "Catch me!" Dogs will do this to one another, too. In all cases, they are looking to signal friendship while also creating a sense of tension, perhaps a battle for an object, or a chase, because dogs understand that play requires the conceit of competition. If you do not fight for the sock, the dog is disappointed. What they are looking for is not the sock itself, but the fun of play-fighting someone for that sock.

It is a principle simple enough for dogs to understand and most humans have a pretty easy time with it, too. But it gets more complicated when we start playing a *cooperative* game, where players are not competing against each other for victory but banding together as a team against the game itself. Everyone wins together or everyone loses together. There has been a vogue for these games in recent years. Let me introduce you to the most famous one.

Matt Leacock's *Pandemic*, published in 2008 by Z-Man Games, was not the first cooperative tabletop game but it popularized the genre in a way no other game had before. In the story of this game, the human race is facing a massive, sudden, global outbreak of infectious disease. Four deadly plagues are ravaging the population, and any one of them could wipe out all of humanity. The players take on the roles of the very few medical experts in the world who are immune to all four pathogens. It falls upon them to discover cures to these diseases and save humanity. No pressure.

Pandemic is remarkable for the sense of urgency and camaraderie it inspires among players, who must constantly balance the short-term need to treat victims and keep outbreaks under control against the long-term need to gather the resources necessary to discover cures. If the players split up and do their own things separately, they are practically guaranteed to lose. As is typically the case with most cooperative game designs, winning depends on teamwork, communication, coordination, and planning.

Each player can see and know everything their teammates see and know. Unlike in some cooperative games (which we'll talk about later), there is no hidden information. When it is your turn, you need to decide what you are going to do. Your teammates can offer suggestions, pointing out risks and options you may not have noticed, and figuring out ways to coordinate their actions with yours. In this way, a group of players working well together can greatly improve its chances of success.

For a lot of people, the prospect of playing a game with someone who is much better at it than they are is not an attractive one. If you are not much of a chess player, for instance, your odds of winning against a grandmaster are so slim that the game hardly feels worthwhile (remember, no uncertainty, no game). But in *Pandemic*, the other players are not your opponents, they are your teammates. In theory, playing with someone who is much better at it than you should be a good thing because she is on your side.

But is it always better? Suppose one player can see more clearly than the others which moves are more likely to lead to victory, and which ones are more likely to cause problems. If she is following the play contract, trying to play as well as she can, she should be doing her best to help the group win by telling her teammates what she sees. If you are about to make a sub-optimal move, she should point out why it is a problem and perhaps suggest a different move you could make, one which would achieve a better result. No harm, right?

Now suppose our expert player does this for all of her teammates. Suppose she does it every single turn. The group may have a better chance of winning but now only one of them is actually playing. The others are reduced from teammates to spectators. They might as well not even be there. Perhaps this reminds you of the junior and senior partners at the imaginary law firm I described a few pages back.

This happens fairly often in co-operative games—often enough to need a name. And so players and designers have dubbed it the *alpha-player problem*. You might also hear it referred to as *quarterbacking*. In a traditional competitive-style game, there is no alpha-player problem because the play contract ensures a natural kind of sustaining tension—everyone is out for his own gain. But in a co-op game, the play contract doesn't always work. In fact, it can cause the game to turn in on itself in ways that aren't even the alpha player's fault.

The alpha has only two options in *Pandemic*, both equally unappealing. If the alpha tells the group what she thinks everyone should do, she takes away her teammates' agency and denies them the chance to play and have fun. But if she remains silent, she violates the play contract by failing to help her teammates to the best of her ability. Option two also makes the game a lot less fun for the alpha player, because she doesn't get the chance to apply herself fully toward victory.

For some players, this makes *Pandemic* a game with no way to have fun. (That includes my co-author Jonathan, who generally avoids cooperative games altogether—largely for this reason.) And yet it is a smash hit, a superstar among modern games, with three expansion sets, eight spinoff titles (as of February 2019), and a super deluxe tenth-anniversary edition that comes in an awesome metal briefcase that looks like a medical kit. How can this be, when the basic precepts everyone must at least tacitly agree to when sitting down to play a game make it impossible for it to deliver a good experience? Well, being clever folks, game players have devised a number of ways to deal with the alpha-player problem.

One easy way to avoid the alpha-player problem is to follow the third precept of the play contract at the expense of the second. That means the alpha just accepts that she is not going to play her absolute best. She allows the others to play the game at their own level, and to win or lose on their own terms. A less paternalistic way of going about this would be for the non-alphas to impose this solution by shushing or otherwise declining advice from the alpha.

To bring the discussion back to the law-firm example we started with, this approach would be like a senior partner deciding that he is going to sacrifice some short-term efficiency on the file the team is working on so that he can train up junior team members.

He is still pursuing an "optimal" result, but "optimal" is now being defined according to a long-term framework that takes larger goals into account such as a firm's need to develop future talent and leadership. In the same way, an alpha player might see it as "optimal" to allow newer players to make mistakes—because it helps them get better through trial and error, thereby helping to keep the gaming group together and lay the groundwork for more fun in future games. (A gaming purist might say that this step serves to break the magic circle because the alpha player must compromise in-game objectives to satisfy the real-world social and psychological needs of other gamers. But as with all forms of doctrinal absolutism, this sort of fundamentalist attitude to gaming serves to make the great the enemy of the good.)

This kind of far-sighted approach becomes a dicey proposition, however, when the stakes are raised. Consider *Pandemic Legacy*, an advanced version of the game in which the components of the game (the board, the cards, tokens and so on) are altered in *permanent* ways as a result of players' in-game decisions. Entire cities can permanently fall to rioting, and characters can become permanently scarred or even die. Events in the game may require the board and the cards to be edited with ink or stickers, or even torn to pieces and thrown away. These developments not only affect whether your team will win the game it is playing this week, but also next week and every other week thereafter. To return to the law-firm analogy, this would be the big make-or-break case for your cash-cow client.

Under these circumstances, how sure are you that you want the alpha player to clam up about what another player should do? The ancient Romans appointed real-life alpha players, whom they called dictators when their territory was invaded by barbarians. They reasoned that a group of squabbling senators, perfectly fine for running things in peacetime, were underqualified when life-and-death decisions needed to be made with no time for debate and discussion: just bring in dictators such as Lucius Quinctius Cincinnatus or Marcus Furius Camillus and do what they say. (Those dudes were alpha AF, as the kids like to say.) Then again, that just gets us into the higher-level problem of who gets to decide which situations require "dictators" and which don't. Certainly, the alpha player herself can't be trusted with that decision—because one of the defining attributes of many alpha players is that they diagnose *every* problem as requiring the intervention of an alpha player.

But good game design can get us around this problem by structuring the game in a way that deprives any one player of the omniscience required to take complete command. In Juan Rodriguez and Fabien Riffaud's macabre World War I-themed card game *The Grizzled* (2015), and Antoine Bauza's award-winning *Hanabi* (2010), for instance, players work together to accomplish a common goal but each has access to information teammates cannot see, and all are severely restricted in their ability to communicate. Without access to the entire picture, no alpha player can know for certain which moves will or will not be beneficial to the team. So everyone has to try his or her best with the limited information they possess.

Another way of dealing with the alpha-player problem in cooperative games is to put players in a time crunch. In Eric M. Lang's alien-invasion resistance epic *XCOM: The Board Game* (2015), Vlaada Chvatil's space-borne comedy of errors *Space Alert* (2008), and Kane Klenko's nail-biter of a bomb disposal game *Fuse* (2015), all information can be shared among all players, in theory. In practice, it is impossible to share more than a few snippets of it because players must make choices within a severely limited amount of time. Potential alphas do not have time to micromanage everyone else. They and all the rest must decide when a piece of information is important enough to be worth expending the group's precious time and attention to share it.

Can this trick of tackling the alpha-player problem by providing players with limited *information* or limited *time* to act on that information be extended to real-world organizational behavior patterns? Definitely. One of the main reasons some bosses micromanage is that they do not have a lot of work on their own desks. Give a boss something to do, and she will tend to give more autonomy to her minions. Likewise, minions who are tired of being told how to tie their shoelaces may rebel against corporate higher-ups by hoarding data within their fiefdoms and throttling the flow of information. The boss cannot micromanage a department she cannot fully survey or understand.

Yet another strategy for tackling the alpha-player problem is to reduce player trust. In Serge Laget and Bruno Cathala's *Shadows Over Camelot* (2005) and Jonathan Gilmour and Isaac Vega's *Dead of Winter* (2015) which I will be going into in some detail in the next chapter, the games are structured in a broadly cooperative way but with an important twist: there is the ever-present possibility that one of the other players may be a secret traitor, trying to sabotage the game and make sure everyone else loses. This means everyone has good reason to treat a potential alpha player's advice with skepticism and make solitary decisions, since the would-be alpha may not have pure intentions. (This approach rather reminds me of the Iron Law of Institutions: people within an institution will always prioritize their own position within that institution over the health of the institution itself. I do not recommend its implementation as a means of improving corporate morale.)

There is one last design-based approach I want to talk about, and although it looks like lazy design on the surface, it is, in fact, one of my favorite strategies for creating cooperative games that can be enjoyed by groups of players with widely divergent skill levels. It is the trick of lowering a game's emotional stakes.

Jason C. Hill's *A Touch of Evil* (2008) is a lighthearted game of Gothic horror in colonial America. Think Sleepy Hollow with the serial numbers filed off. The cards are illustrated with photographs of people who look like they must be friends of the design team, wearing questionably period-accurate costumes and hamming it up for the camera. It has the feel of a community theatre production put on by people with more enthusiasm than skill. While this puts some players off, other gamers—myself included—find it charming. The people in those photos are having so much darned fun.

This lighthearted attitude carries through to the game's design as well. It is wacky and random and intended to be played casually. Because strategy plays a relatively minor role in determining the outcome, nobody really minds if someone makes a suboptimal move. There are limits to this, of course: if somebody's moves run directly contrary to the group's goals, or if they break immersion in the story, the game still suffers. But there is plenty of room in this style of cooperative game for players to disagree over how best to accomplish something without anyone feeling the need to take charge, play dictator, and destroy the Roman Republic.

Ultimately, the best solution to the alpha-player problem isn't based on picking the right rules. It is based on picking the right teammates. In a game of alpha players, nobody is an alpha player. Similarly, if everyone is new to a game, players can stumble happily along as a team, making mistakes together and learning lessons about how to win on the next attempt.

Even a table that contains both expert players and neophytes does not have to fall victim to the alpha-player problem. I am not a huge fan of the original *Pandemic* because I am insufferably alpha (at the tabletop, that is), and I do not like having to choose between being passively unhelpful or actively ruining my friends' enjoyment by telling them their correct moves. So I was worried when I set out on the epic multi-game campaign of *Pandemic Legacy* with two friends who made for a bit of a mixed group. One member does not have much confidence at games, and one is perhaps even more alpha than

I am. But, strangely, that initially unpromising chemistry turned out to be our key to success.

Because our group had not one but two alphas, we would end up arguing about this or that move, trying to persuade the another that one were correct and the other was mistaken. In effect, we were performing for our third teammate, who, after hearing both sides, would feel well-informed and reasonably confident in making decisions.

* * *

This is not an airport-rack business book to show you how to get the most out of your employees, improve staff morale, or reduce friction within your organization. But playing games really can provide important lessons for people running companies. In particular, cooperative games such as *Pandemic* teach us that group dynamics can get more complicated, not less when people are trying to co-operate rather than compete. This is important because most businesses, NGOs, government agencies, social clubs and even families can be thought of in some way as *cooperative* projects, even if real life tends to lack the well-defined rules and victory conditions you would find in a cooperative board game.

Like players in a cooperative game, close colleagues may end up struggling with the balance between the ruthless pursuit of short-term performance and the long-term effort to enhance their colleagues' skills and sense of engagement. Too much of the former, and the company becomes a haven for alphas but alienates everybody else. Too much of the latter, and the company might have trouble satisfying its clients—even as it develops a great reputation for in-house vocational mentorship.

In most organizations, there are unwritten rules that govern the desired mix, much like the play contract at the tabletop. These rules go a long way toward defining an organization's culture. And if you are going to join up, you will probably want to make sure that your own values are congruent—whether it is a multinational corporation making widgets or just a few friends gathered around a game board, trying to save the human race from extinction.

CHAPTER SIX

The Zombie Survivor's Dilemma

(Joan Moriarity: Lessons from Dead of Winter*)*

ZOMBIES WERE HUGE A few years back. From movie theatres to small screens to tabletops, shuffling hordes of undead were everywhere and the message contained within their stories was remarkably consistent across all media: humans are the true monsters.

Games about zombies tend to fall into one of two thematic categories: those about fighting zombies, and those about dealing with life in a world filled with zombies. The majority are firmly in the former category. Typically, these are tactical games about managing health and supplies (especially ammunition) among a mixed bag of post-apocalyptic survivors. The cathartic release of mowing down hordes of undead can be satisfying, but the zombies in those games might just as easily be orcs or Nazis or any other generic baddie. As a result, these games tend not to offer much that is thematically unique.

The second zombie-game category is less common and far more demanding of players. In the vein of stories such as *The Walking*

Dead (TV or comics, take your pick) and novels such as Stephen King's *The Stand* and Justin Cronin's *Passage* trilogy, these survival games put players in the shoes of characters pushed to their absolute limits, with notions of traditional morality pitted against the need to survive.

No other game evokes this grim subgenre more powerfully than *Dead of Winter*, created by Jonathan Gilmour and Isaac Vega, and published by Plaid Hat Games in 2014. In this deeply immersive game, each player controls a small group of zombie apocalypse survivors who have banded together to form a colony. The shared hope is that strength in numbers will allow everyone to make it through a lethal cold snap without succumbing to the killing cold, or falling prey to walking corpses in the abandoned streets. The colony has established a fortified warehouse as its base, and now must work as a team to accomplish common goals such as collecting a certain amount of body parts from slain zombies to develop a vaccine for the zombie plague, or gathering up a certain amount of fuel to move the endangered colony to a new location.

As in most cooperative games, the players must communicate, coordinate, and plan together to have any hope of success. But in a cruel and thematically perfect twist, each player also has a secret goal he must accomplish in order to win, and these private goals are always bad for the group. For example, one player might secretly be a junkie who needs to hoard medicines, which are something the rest of the colony desperately needs. Or one player might have witnessed horrors that have left her convinced that humanity deserves to be punished for what it has done to this world, and so she cannot win the game unless at least three of the story's protagonists have died. Yet in order for any individual player to win the game, both the public goal *and* a secret private goal must be accomplished. This creates exactly the kind of tension that makes the most intense zombie fiction, like *The Stand* or *The Passage,* so compelling.

(Games such as *Dead of Winter*, in which players must both co-operate and compete, are part of a rising subgenre that I refer to as "co-op-etitive," a fun word to say that, I confess, has not caught on). You can also see the mash-up structure in the 1990 cult classic *The Republic of Rome*, in which players command factions in ancient Roman society. Players win that game if their noble families accumulate more money, prestige and influence than their opponents. But if this competition for riches becomes so intense that it causes everyone to ignore the larger needs of Rome, the barbarians march in, or the citizens revolt and *everyone* loses. Much as nobles did historically in the late Roman republic players tend to apply just enough resources and attention to the health of the empire to keep it alive, while devoting most of their time to brazen self-aggrandizement.)

Here is a typical scenario in *Dead of Winter*. One of your fellow players has sent a survivor to scrounge through the police station to find weapons. A large group of zombies has unexpectedly surrounded the scavenger. One of your own survivors is at the nearby hospital searching for medical supplies, and they could draw some undead away from the police station, which would keep the other survivor alive, at least for a while. However, doing so would compromise your own search for desperately needed medicine. What should you do?

The game is designed to engineer recurring moments like this, which lead to slippery moral slopes. When the game starts, everyone co-operates. As the plot develops, each player is drawn more and more toward self-interest. If you have already done the selfish thing once, does it matter so much if you do it again? And each time you do something to further your own private goal, you give another clue about the nature of that goal, and so have less reason to hide your true intentions in the future. Your fellow players might be forgiven for feeling like you are trying to sabotage the game and make everyone lose.

Here's the real danger. Every time you play *Dead of Winter*, there is about a 50-50 chance that one of the players will receive a secret goal that actually *does* require them to sabotage the game completely and make everyone lose. While this happens only about half the time, everyone worries about it *every* time. There is no way to know who the betrayer is, or even if there is a betrayer at all, unless it is you, in which case you need to do whatever is necessary to make sure that no one finds out until it is too late.

The atmosphere of paranoia and distrust created by this bit of game design perfectly mirrors the drama on display in the most brutal zombie stories. It also draws upon the existential fear that infuses that wide swath of horror and science fiction centered on the zombie genre—but which also includes such specimens as *Battlestar Galactica*, the *Terminator* movies, *Invasion of the Body Snatchers*, and arguably even *The Manchurian Candidate*—where our society has been infiltrated by secret look-alikes who are either robots, aliens, conspirators, or carriers of disease. In the ensuing hysteria, innocents are often targeted while the true evildoer slips free.

The last time I played *Dead of Winter*, there were three of us in the game. Apart from a few minor peccadilloes, none of us appeared to be to sabotaging our mission so we were fairly certain that we did not have a betrayer among us. We had nearly achieved our common objective and I had nearly achieved my private goal. I just needed to play two more cards, one for each goal. As it turned out, I only had one such card, and I could use it only once.

If I used that card to complete the public goal, I would fail my private goal and lose the game. If I used it for my private goal, the public goal would fail and I would lose the game but the other players would lose with me, resulting in a three-way tie. You might think that the thing to do in this case would be to ensure that if I could not win, nobody else would either. That would be a fittingly dark end to our little story and not at all inappropriate for the post-apocalyptic genre. But there were other considerations at play.

In the moment, I was reminded of the famous psychological experiment known as the Prisoner's Dilemma, which itself is almost a game. Two criminals have been arrested for the same crime, and they are interrogated in separate rooms. Each is offered a lighter sentence if he rats out his accomplice. If you betray your accomplice while the accomplice remains silent, the accomplice goes to prison for three years and you are free. If you betray each other, you both go to prison for two years. If you both stay silent, you both go to prison for one year. While the game is not that interesting when a single round is played in isolation, it becomes more intriguing if you play multiple rounds sequentially—with each player reacting, either positively or negatively, to the decisions made by the other player in preceding rounds. Sometimes, you wind up in positive cycles of trust. In other cases, you get negative cycles of punishment and revenge.

In 1980, a group of computer scientists set out to find an ideal strategy for optimizing results against an opponent through multiple, iterative rounds of this little game. They pitted a variety of computer programs against each other in a tournament. Each of these programs was created with a particular set of instructions that constituted its strategy, and each program played two hundred games of the Prisoner's Dilemma against all of the other programs. Some programs were coded for revenge; others for turning the other cheek; others for some mixture of the two. At the end of the tournament, the total amount of assigned prison time would be tallied up and the program that had served least would be declared the winner.

Some of the programs were quite complex, taking into account all kinds of variables in their efforts to guess how their counterparts would behave. The program that won the tournament, however, was one of the simplest. It was called "Tit For Tat." On its first round with any given opponent, it would remain silent. After that, it would always take the same action its opponent had taken on the previous round. This was part of a larger trend among the best-performing programs: they played *nice*. They would not betray their opponent unless they were betrayed first.

The game design of the Prisoner's Dilemma provides a short-term incentive for players to be cruel because betraying your accomplice always gives you a lighter sentence than you would get for staying silent, regardless of what the other player does. Assuming they betray you, you will get two years if you betray them and three if you remain silent. Assuming they keep quiet, you will get a year if you keep quiet as well, but you will go free if you betray.

As you play more rounds, the dynamic changes completely. There is now an incentive to be kind because, over time, co-operating will result in less total time served between the two of you. If nobody betrays, you each get one year, so two years total. If one of you betrays, the total is three years, and if you both betray, the total is four. So if you are looking at the long term, say the two hundred consecutive games played in the above-described tournament, you need to convince the other player to co-operate with you as often as possible. In practice, it seems the most effective way to do that is to proactively lead them to expect that you will play nice as well.

This is very different from the mind games Jonathan talked about in his earlier chapter on *Chinatown* and *No Thanks!* The Ultimatum Game is about deterring people from being jerks in a zero-sum scoring environment where your victory means my defeat, and my victory means your defeat. The Prisoner's Dilemma is about signaling cooperation in a contest that is not zero-sum, where my victories can be good for you and my losses can be bad for you, at least in the long term.

This points to one of the reasons why the characters in post-apocalyptic fiction tend to be so horrible to one another. In a functioning society where there is a good chance people will eventually cross paths again with those they have wronged, even a selfish person can see the benefits of co-operation. In a destroyed world where society is effectively gone, and justice (or what passes for justice) is meted out with shotgun and crowbar, two people who do not expect to ever see each another again might feel they can safely ignore the consequences for screwing someone over and taking their stuff.

Although this might account for the behavior of fictional characters in fictional worlds, observation of real-world human behavior tells a different story. In the aftermath of natural disasters and other horrifying situations, humans do not magically transform into jerks. In fact, it is often quite the opposite. Hurricanes, earthquakes, and other apocalyptic events can bring out the best in people, inspiring us to extraordinary feats of heroism and selflessness. Pro-social behavior, mutual sympathy and support made it possible for humans to conquer this planet. Zombie fiction almost always gets this wrong, because it has to. A zombie story that presented an accurate depiction of human behavior *in extremis* would be too uplifting to get funded by HBO or Netflix. What would that kind of show even look like?

Why, it might resemble that game of *Dead of Winter* I was talking about earlier. Let me tell you how it ended.

My most rational short-term, in-game choice, as already noted, was to make sure we all lost together. That would effectively result in a tie game. But I had spent the last ninety minutes fighting alongside my friends, not only against the corpses out to feast on our brains but also against the pitiless elements as well. They had trusted me, and I had trusted them. In spite of all that was arrayed against us, we had survived, and we were close to our goal. If their fears had led them to treat me like a suspected betrayer, if they had approached every interaction with me wondering what ulterior motive I could have for whatever I was doing, if they had treated me poorly, I may well have thought nothing of condemning all of us to death in the empty, frozen streets of a world without hope. But they had not. And so I decreed that my own little group of survivors would sacrifice themselves to give the others a chance. I lost, and they won.

I did not mind in the slightest. I did not feel like I had betrayed the play contract I mentioned in the *Pandemic* chapter because an immersive, story-driven game such as *Dead of Winter* isn't an abstract game like dominoes or backgammon. In gaming moments like that, I come to realize that the play contract has to make allowances for the need to make choices that are consistent with the feel of a compelling imaginary world, including its ethical dimension. As Jonathan explains in his chapter on *Advanced Squad Leader*, some games produce such rich narratives that the protection of the narrative's integrity becomes its own in-game goal. Neither of my opponents felt frustrated that I had not provided them with enough opposition to make the game interesting. They were saddened by my loss but heartened by what it meant.

There is no guarantee that this would be the case with every play group. Zombie stories are filled with hopelessness and despair. If you sat down to play *Dead of Winter* with a group of players who had come to the table to channel the sheer nihilism of that world for an evening, my actions would have seemed nonsensical—perhaps even disrespectful. *We put all this time and energy into playing this game with you, and yet when the time came to do the right thing and stab us in the back, you took the low road and let us live. How dare you?*

But just as different actors may choose to bring out different facets of the same character, so too can gamers bring out different themes of the same game. In the grim darkness of that deadly winter, we had defied the odds, defied genre conventions, and chosen to heed the better angels of our nature. My people were lost, devoured by the same vast legions of undead who in time would likely annihilate this planet and all who yet live upon it. But though they may have eaten my brain, I resolved that they would never consume my soul.

CHAPTER SEVEN

The Game That Explains Everything

(Jonathan Kay: Lessons from Monopoly*)*

IMAGINE YOU ARE IN the late stages of a game of *Monopoly*, battling it out against a lone remaining opponent. You each control a bunch of expensive properties, all loaded with hotels. Both of you also are cash poor, with no spare properties left to mortgage. Every roll of the dice carries high stakes. If your opponent lands on one of your hotels, the only way he can pay the rent will be to sell off his own hotels at a 50 percent discount (because that is how the rules of *Monopoly* work), and vice versa. Which means that the first player who lands on an opponent's hotel will not just lose a lot of money: he will also lose the assets he needs to earn that money back. In real life, the analogy would be the poor worker in Victorian Britain who, unable to pay his debts, goes to debtor's prison which further compromises his ability to earn a livelihood, and so pushes his family deeper into destitution.

"Well, that's capitalism," you might say. Perhaps. We will get to that later. For now, I want to emphasize that this aspect of *Monopoly*—the poor get poorer, while the rich get richer—is not only typical of laissez-faire economics. It is also characteristic of a certain dynamic observed in nature, engineering, and human relationships, one that mathematicians sometimes describe as unstable equilibrium.

Take a simple physical metaphor: a marble resting at the bottom of a salad bowl is going to exhibit a *stable* equilibrium in that small movements in any direction will push the marble up against the walls of the bowl, and the marble will roll back towards its start position, also known as its equilibrium point. If the salad bowl is turned upside down, however, and the marble is placed at the top of it, the marble will exhibit an unstable equilibrium: even if the marble is balanced perfectly on top of the bowl, and so remains temporarily motionless, a nudge in any direction will lead to a feedback loop whereby the marble rolls off the bowl, moving slowly at first and then accelerating downward. In general, a stable equilibrium tends to correct itself, restoring the balance of offsetting forces that held it in check to begin with; an unstable equilibrium tends to accelerate off in one direction or another until the system in some way collapses or reaches a different stable equilibrium.

Now let us return to *Monopoly*. You and your imaginary opponent are moving your tokens around the board, seeking to avoid one another's hotels. In a way, you each inhabit an economic state analogous to the marble sitting on top of that salad bowl. All you need is a single initial nudge toward poverty and a cascade will begin, pushing you further and further down.

Monopoly is not the only game in which this kind of phenomenon plays out. The same thing happens in chess: if your opponent blunders away a bishop or a rook, she not only has one fewer piece available to attack your king, she also has one fewer pieces available to defend her remaining pieces. It becomes more likely that one of those pieces will also be lost, and then another, and another, until her side collapses completely. This is why expert chess players sometimes will resign a game after losing just a single pawn because they know that top-flight opponents will exploit any tiny advantage so as to create larger and larger advantages until the game ends in a rout. This is why chess is such a tense game.

Stability theory has enormous real-world ramifications. As an engineer in the 1990s, I spent a lot of my time figuring out how to ensure that the systems I designed, whether software or hardware, would not go haywire if they were nudged in one direction or another. In some cases, solutions can be obvious and low-tech. Remember those old toys called Weebles? The reason "Weebles wobble but they don't fall down" is that the toy's weight is bottom-loaded. Similarly, a sailboat in a windstorm also can exhibit a stable equilibrium: the more the wind pushes the sailboat over, the less sail height is presented to the wind, meaning that less rotational force is applied to the boat—a true self-correcting system (within certain environmental limits).

But in other cases, ensuring stability in an engineering system requires high-tech methods. Think of a Segway scooter, a system that, like a marble sitting atop an inverted bowl, very much *looks* like it should collapse if nudged from the front or the rear. (Engineers call it the "inverted pendulum" problem.) The system achieves stability only through the ingenious use of hidden electric motors, gyroscopes and tilt sensors.

I went through a period of life when I was fixated on the nature of dynamical systems—including the chaotic dynamical systems represented by certain forms of fractal geometry, which I discovered through James Gleick's ground-breaking 1987 book, *Chaos: Making a New Science*. It is a rich area of mathematical modeling that I am giving only the most superficial treatment in this chapter, but you do not have to be a mathematician or engineer to appreciate the way certain systems gravitate toward either stability or instability. All you have to do is play board games.

Imagine, for instance, a game in which there was a built-in stabilizing mechanic that actually *penalized* a player for being in the lead? Well, guess what: I just described the "robber" in *Catan*. Of course, there is no rule that says the robber has to be placed in a way that targets the winning player. But that is what usually happens (except when the winning player herself is repositioning the robber), since everyone has a built-in incentive to take down the top dog. That is one of the reasons why *Catan* is less likely than *Monopoly* to send people away pouting: the game mechanics are designed in a way that helps underdogs.

Similarly, in the epic 1970s-era war game *Civilization*, the losing player gets the benefit of moving her troops last in any game turn (a huge advantage). And in *Power Grid*, described in chapter 2, the losing player gets to bid first on available fuel sources. Think of these elements as the gameplay equivalent of the sensor-driven motors in a Segway that push back against gravity and keep the thing from falling over.

It is not hard to see how *Monopoly* could be retrofitted in the same way. Indeed, the game already has a few stabilizing elements such as the Community Chest card that reads "You are assessed for street repairs: pay $40 per house and $115 per hotel you own." (There is another version of this card in the Chance deck which assesses costs for houses and hotels at $25 and $100 respectively.) If you wanted to make a more "stable" version of *Monopoly*, all you would have to do is add more cards like this to the decks, and perhaps increase the assessed amounts. You could also stipulate that the person who draws this card does not pay the assessed fees to the bank but instead pays it to the player with the fewest houses and hotels. Or you could make it progressively more expensive for players to buy houses and hotels depending on how many houses and hotels they already own. Or you could stipulate that the winning player does not get two hundred dollars every time he passes go. I could provide more examples, but you get the picture. These rules all serve to add a stabilizing dose of the-rich-get-soaked or the-poor-get-a-helping-hand to the game's naturally unstable rich-get-richer dynamic.

What I am describing here is not just a way to fix *Monopoly*. It is a way to fix one of the basic problems with capitalism as we now experience it in the era of globalized winner-take-all electronic commerce. A hundred years ago, a successful store owner could put other store owners in his neighborhood out of business. In 2019, Amazon and Alibaba are pushing whole bricks-and-mortar retail *sectors* into bankruptcy on a global level. Meanwhile, Google and Facebook are vacuuming up the lion's share of web advertising. As *The New Republic* reported in late 2018, monopolies now penetrate almost every sector: "Two companies make 64 percent of American diapers; one company builds 52 percent of America's mobile homes; two companies produce 78 percent of its corn seeds; and one company assembles 61 percent of syringes."

As many economists have noted, the resultant income inequality is not just a threat to our egalitarian ideals. It is a threat to capitalism itself since the health of the free market always will depend on a viable middle class that supplies both demand and labor to a mass retail economy. (Poor people do not have enough money to buy much. And the super-rich spend a very small percentage of their income on goods and services.) A game of *Monopoly* ends when one player has all the money and everyone else is bankrupt. But a human society is not something that you fold up and put back in the box. It is not supposed to *end*. So you need a way to stabilize the economic dynamic, to make sure the rider doesn't fall off the Segway, to keep the marble on top of the upside-down salad bowl. Otherwise, you get depressions, financial crises, and even revolutions.

Critics of capitalism often decry the "greed" that animates successful entrepreneurs. The real problem, however, is not the amount of money made by people at the top; it is the systematic suppression of people at the bottom. The real-life equivalent of the *Monopoly* player who has to mortgage all his money-making assets to pay his debts is the hand-to-mouth day laborer who, unable to pay his car insurance, loses his car and, unable to drive to his job, is unable to pay his rent. The villain here is not necessarily the avarice of the banker who loaned this poor fellow his money in the first place. It is the unstable dynamic of a system that mercilessly drives some people down to the bottom through a succession of cascading misfortunes.

To experience the board game version of this kind of misery vortex in *Monopoly* is to appreciate the advantages of the welfare state, which, when it is functioning properly, does not just take money from rich people and give it to poor people. It also softens the iterative feedback dynamics within the system so as to ensure that minor nudges—a lost job, a criminal conviction, a divorce, a medical setback—do not create feedback effects that ultimately produce a full-blown personal catastrophe. Job training, public health care, a humane justice system, community housing and support for single mothers are examples of programs that can achieve that effect.

It is also possible to take inspiration from pre-capitalist societies, which operated under very different economic feedback mechanisms. One of the reasons why the Indigenous societies I will be discussing in the upcoming chapter on *Greenland* were more economically egalitarian than our own is that it often was impossible for the most successful hunters to consume all the meat, blubber and bone they harvested from a whale or walrus. If they did not share it with the clan, a lot of it would simply rot (a fact that is actually modeled within that game).

* * *

It has been almost thirty years since I devoted myself to the academic examination of stability theory and dynamical systems. Regardless, it is the sort of subject that, once studied, can never be forgotten. And this kind of analysis continues to color every aspect of my outlook on life—including the way I think of the future of our species.

Consider climate change, perhaps *the* most important issue facing the planet. One of the reasons why climate modeling is so complicated is that our climate is, in some respects, an unstable dynamical system that, if pushed hard in one direction (say, by massive surges in atmospheric carbon dioxide concentrations) can cause a cascade of feedback effects that compound the initial perturbation, and send the whole atmosphere into a radically different equilibrium state.

Understanding the nature of these "feedback effects" is critical if we are to understand the threat. To take one example, a warming earth causes glaciers to melt, thereby decreasing the amount of surface snow and ice that reflect solar radiation back into the atmosphere. Thanks to this sort of positive feedback mechanism, a warmer earth keeps getting warmer, melting more ice, absorbing more solar radiation and so on until Miami Beach is chest-deep in water.

Or consider war, that ancient scourge of human civilization. "Firepower and heavy defensive armament—not merely the ability but also the desire to deliver fatal blows and then steadfastly to endure, without retreat, any counter-response—have always been the trademark of Western armies," wrote Victor Davis Hanson in his 1989 classic, *The Western Way of War: Infantry Battle in Classical Greece.* The reason why these ancient battles were so decisive— "a single, magnificent collision of infantry," as Hanson described the archetype—is that the brand of warfare waged by Greek phalanxes (and, later, Roman maniples) typically followed the same fundamentally unstable equilibrium you see in chess, even when the adversaries were, at the dawn of battle, evenly matched.

When soldiers lost their nerve because some aspect of the battle initially went poorly, or because they were surrounded by a flanking maneuver, they sometimes would turn and flee, progressively throwing the soldiers around them into greater states of confusion and terror, and exposing everybody to complete slaughter. This domino effect was on bloody display at Adrianople, for instance, in 378 AD when Gothic cavalry surrounded and hacked to death a larger force of Roman troops, thereby setting the stage for the fall of the Western half of the empire. Something similar happened six centuries earlier, at Cannae, where fifty thousand Carthaginian troops commanded by Hannibal massacred a force of eighty-six thousand Romans almost to the last man. In the first two years of World War II, the German army performed roughly analogous feats of arms by using columns of blitzkrieg-ing tanks to encircle and defeat Polish, French and Russian defenders.

This helps explain why these conflicts are such popular themes for war games. Unstable battle dynamics tend to produce exciting, dramatic results. World War II, with its highly kinetic battles, has inspired more war games than any other war. Indeed, the 1942 Battle of Stalingrad alone (which ended with the encirclement and massacre of the German Sixth Army) has been the subject of at least seventy published board game titles.

Compare this with World War I, which is a relatively rare subject for board game designers. The reason is obvious: the hyper-stable trench-warfare dynamic that governed the conflict makes gameplay predictable and boring. In World War II, the availability of massed tanks and air power meant that an attacker could apply enormous striking power in a way that could easily overwhelm an enemy's localized defenses. In World War I, on the other hand, the reliance on trenches and machine guns created the opposite dynamic: most attacks resulted in hideous casualties for the attacker and few for the defender. Any perturbation to the battlefield dynamic would almost inevitably end with a reversion to the status quo.

Does this suggest some sort of simple, linear relationship between battlefield dynamical instability and gaming fun? No, because at some point, a military dynamic becomes so unstable that it does not really lend itself to any satisfying form of recreational simulation. It is notable, for instance, that hyper-modern forms of warfare, especially those involving standoff missile systems or nuclear payloads, are not popular themes among war-gamers. If you can annihilate whole countries with the push of a button, the game becomes a simple race to see who can push the button first. There have been some good games produced on the Cold War theme (such as *Twilight Struggle*), yet these tend to avoid the apocalyptic military aspect and instead focus on espionage, geopolitics, diplomacy, trade and scientific competition.

In gaming, as in some parts of life, there is always going to be a sweet spot between perfectly stable and perfectly unstable system dynamics. The rich-get-richer aspect of *Monopoly* may produce bitterness and social friction. But on the other hand, no one would want to play a perfectly socialistic version of the game, in which all income is distributed equitably, no one ever goes bankrupt, and the game never ends. Likewise, a real-life economy in which there are no winners and no losers would not work because, as twentieth-century experiments with communisms showed us, an economy in which hard work yields no personal benefits is an economy in which no one does hard work.

* * *

Board games take inspiration from real life. That does not mean they always reflect the values and preferences we exercise in our real-life capacities as workers, family members, friends and political actors. Some of us may be drawn to the cutthroat dynamical instability of *Monopoly* because it makes for exciting game play, while also recognizing the fact that real life has to follow different rules because humans have more complex and urgent needs than game tokens.

Even so, the dynamics that govern *Monopoly* (not to mention chess, *Civilization*, *Power Grid*, *Catan* and every other game mentioned in this book) can help us understand how much of the character of our societies is embedded in—and dictated by—the dynamical feedback processes encoded in our economy and laws.

If you want to improve the moral character of a society, you do not necessarily have to change the way people think and feel. Sometimes, all you have to do is fiddle with the rules that govern what happens every time they pass Go.

CHAPTER EIGHT

The Stupid Free Parking Rule

(Joan Moriarity: Lessons from Monopoly*)*

Unlike every other chapter in this book, this one is written in a way that presupposes that you have played the game under discussion at some point in your lifetime. Also for most readers, there is a strong likelihood that this presupposition is true. But if you have never played *Monopoly*, do feel free to skip to the next chapter and consider yourself fortunate in the eyes of game snobs like myself, who look down their noses at *Monopoly* as an antiquated, obsolete, and best-forgotten relic of a dark and grim age of game design (notwithstanding my co-author's amusing claim in the previous chapter that analyzing the game's dynamic somehow will help us save capitalism from itself).

This chapter also will be unusual in the sense that I will be diving into the nitty gritty of the game's rules—because there is one particular rule that I want to put at the center of the discussion. Yes, it is The Stupid Free Parking Rule. Yes, I am going to keep calling it the Stupid Free Parking Rule, and I sincerely hope the name catches on because that's what it is. (And I am using the word "rule" in the loosest possible sense because there is, in fact, no such rule—which is a big part of the problem.)

* * *

For many game nerds, discussions of the "right way" to play *Monopoly* are old hat. But for the benefit of everyone else, I offer this brief summary. According to the rules as written, the "Free Parking" space does not do anything. It is just a free space. It has no other function than to act as something for your token to sit on. The words "Free Parking" might as well be "Smoke 'Em If You Got 'Em."

But most people who play *Monopoly* do not play according to the rules as written. Whenever they have to pay money for landing on Income Tax or Luxury Tax, or because of a penalty assessed by a Chance or Community Chest card, they put the forfeited money in the middle of the board (instead of paying it to the bank—as the rules clearly require them to do). Then whenever somebody lands on Free Parking, they collect that money as a prize. It is not clear how this tradition arose, but for many, it is simply how the game is played.

Perhaps the only *Monopoly*-related topic that has been beaten to death among gaming nerds more severely than The Stupid Free Parking Rule is the question of why *Monopoly* is a "bad" game (again, notwithstanding my co-author's insistence that it is the secret to understanding the cosmos). So, again, a brief summary: it is too long, too heavily based on chance, offers few meaningful decisions to make (in most cases, the right thing to do is clear to anyone who paid attention in math class), an it eliminates players one at a time, leaving them with nothing to do except become bored and embittered while the other players finish. Are we having fun yet?

The Stupid Free Parking Rule worsens these design problems. Luxury Tax and Income Tax, and other such penalties, are there to extract currency from the game, pushing the players toward bankruptcy and the game toward a conclusion. When that currency floods back into the game through the Free Parking space, it makes an already long ordeal much longer and more random. Over the years, on all the many occasions I have pointed this out, people almost always think for a moment, nod, and agree. This is not some kind of mysterious game knowledge known only to a few.

The real mystery is this: when it is so clear that The Stupid Free Parking Rule makes the game worse, why is it that so many people insist on using it, especially when it clearly violates the rules of the game as written? Chess players follow the rules of the games they play. No one says, "Hey, why don't we play that when you take your opponent's queen with a bishop, he gets a free move with two of his pawns." What makes *Monopoly* so different?

Discovering the truth behind this mystery has been more difficult than you might imagine. Here I present to you the fruits of my exhaustive research: nine hypothetical reasons why people use the Stupid Free Parking Rule (and one real one).

1. Monopoly is hard on friendships and families, so giving players free money helps keep things calm.

My inner snob desperately wants to tell you how adorable it is that people think *Monopoly* ruins friendships. But I will skip over that because my chapter on *Scattergories*, presented later in this book, puts this problem in context by showing you what a *real* relationship-busting game looks like. Nevertheless, for argument's sake, let us take this idea at face value. *Monopoly* is a capricious game. Players can gain or lose huge sums of cash according to the fall of the dice. It can be frustrating to lose most of your money because of an unlucky roll, more so because you will probably have to hand that money over to your smug opponent across the table—who will almost certainly spend that money building yet more houses and hotels, thereby pushing along the death spiral we all read about in the previous chapter. But here's the thing: there is no guarantee that the Free Parking money will actually go to players who need a handout. It's just as likely the cash will go to the winning player so he can use it as pocket change.

2. It allows a player who has fallen behind to catch up.

Think of this as a close variant of Rationale No. 1, above: For some players, it is less about peace than *justice*. For these *Monopoly* Justice Warriors, there is an idealized outcome by which the Free Parking jackpot will go to the person who needs it most. By the process of magical thinking, they just assume this will be what happens. But to repeat the point discussed above, the prize is not guaranteed to go to the poorest or unluckiest player. Those who cite this as their reason for using The Stupid Free Parking Rule probably know that, on some level, they are imagining into existence a sort of *Monopoly* God who makes sure that the prize goes to the neediest soul. Which brings us to reason number three.

3. The Free Parking rule is good, but only if I land on it.

Here we have a somewhat more honest expression of the appeal of this rule. People who buy lottery tickets or play slot machines can easily envision themselves winning the jackpot, and the seduction of this vision tricks their brains into seeing a win as more probable than it really is. You've heard the saying that working-class Americans see themselves not as an exploited proletariat but as temporarily embarrassed millionaires? The prevalence of The Stupid Free Parking Rule helps demonstrate the truth of this.

If you are playing *Monopoly* and you just handed over your last seventy-five bucks to the hated Luxury Tax, you could be forgiven for jumping at a chance to win it back at the Free Parking space. Yes, there is a strong chance that one of your opponents will get the money instead, but in that moment, risk analysis may not be foremost in your mind. If people didn't love throwing good money after bad, no casino would remain in business.

4.   It adds an element of surprise

In a game as dull as Monopoly, where geological ages can pass without anything interesting happening, anything that adds some kind of excitement to the proceedings is treated as a welcome diversion. The Stupid Free Parking Rule introduces periods of rising and falling tension to *Monopoly*. Whenever a player approaches the space, players lean forward in their seats, a little farther each time as the jackpot grows and grows. The tension builds until at last somebody takes the prize and the entire table feels a rush of emotion (*negative* emotions for most of the players), and the cycle begins afresh.

This has little to do with the actual game, of course, which is supposed to be about monopolizing tracts of real estate. It is as though a regular by-the-book *Monopoly* game were occasionally interrupted by a side game of bingo. This is what people are talking about when they say The Stupid Free Parking Rule adds "fun." And to give them their due, it can indeed be argued that bingo is more fun than *Monopoly*.

5.   How else can anyone afford to develop their properties?

Here is another design-based rationale for The Stupid Free Parking Rule. Putting houses and hotels on your properties, especially on the expensive half of the board where rent is highest, can be prohibitively expensive. For many players, developing is the most enjoyable part of the game. Those chunks of green and red plastic are some of the most appealing bits in the box; and without the additional currency provided by the occasional Free Parking jackpot, few players will accrue enough cash to use them.

But even if you accept the premise here—that some artifice is necessary to speed up players' development of properties—why would you introduce that artifice in a way that is neither fair nor systematic? Why not just introduce a house rule that gives everyone a 50 percent discount on all houses and hotels?

6. It does not make sense for there to be a space on the board that does nothing.

The idea that every space on the board ought to do something makes some intuitive sense. In films and television, the expectation is that every scene is there for a reason. Yet in music, the rests (spaces between notes) do serve a purpose and can be powerfully effective (think of how different the Queen classic "We Will Rock You" would be without the pause after each set of stomps and claps. In visual art, areas of blank (or "negative") space can have a similarly striking effect. Even in games, players can achieve a lot by *omission* as well as commission. A Poker player's decision not to bet a close hand can win them a tournament.

Still, it is admittedly weird that every space in *Monopoly* does something except Free Parking (and the "Just Visiting" bit of the Jail space, but never mind that). And so I get why it throws people off: Why should there be just this one space that does nothing?

My own answer would be: because *Monopoly* is a poorly designed game that was conceived and created before the modern age of rigorous play testing. But I would also argue that if The Stupid Free Parking Rule is conceived as a means to fix this defect, it is akin to the cure that's worse than the disease.

7. People will get upset if we don't play it that way

Uh, are you serious? Everybody knows that's not how you play Monopoly. Everybody knows you put the money in the middle, and then when somebody lands on Free Parking they take it. Why are we even having this conversation? What? Rulebook? Are you fucking serious?

Players adopting this line of reasoning do not typically go further in their explanations. If presented with a copy of this book open to this chapter, they might point to some of the other reasons (especially Rationales No. 4 or 5) and say "Thats totally what I meant." Ultimately, they want The Stupid Free Parking Rule in the game because That Is The Way Things Are Done.

We all know people who become impossible to bear if we do not play a game *their* way. If even one of the players at your table is going to make a big deal of it and make life miserable for everyone else, it is probably best to let them prevail—and remind yourself that you need to expand your circle of gaming friends.

8. People who see Free Parking as nothing more than a free space lack imagination

This is a more high-flown variation on Rationale No. 8. To go off script, to play according to your own rules, to throw away the rulebook and do your own thing—that does have a certain rebellious appeal, doesn't it? Charming, roguish characters in our favorite stories bend the rules to get the job done and they are freakin' cool, right? Do you want to be Han Solo—or the Death Star security officer quizzing him over the intercom about his "operating number"?

To which I say, "fair enough." After all, as I noted in chapter 3, *Life* wouldn't be fun for many LGBT players if you couldn't bend the rules around pink and blue. But when your rebellion takes the form of doing the same thing almost everyone else does—including your parents—just exactly how rebellious or cool are you? And, ultimately, a game snob might argue, the very act of playing *Monopoly* shows you lack the imagination and initiative required to explore new—and better—games.

9. Screw the bank, we should get that money

Here is an interesting variation on the rebellion argument. In modern board games, whenever there is a common pile of game pieces that any player might need to use during play, it is usually called "the supply" or something equally innocuous. However, the common supply of money that players give to and take from as they play *Monopoly* has a different name, a loaded word: "the bank." For many players, that bit of jargon makes all the difference in the world. It is not a neutral repository in their eyes. It is a sinister, greedy organization that exists to extract wealth from hard working people. The idea that we as players could collectively refuse to let the bank have that money by putting it into our own private raffle can be a satisfying conceit, even if our opponents end up benefiting from it. Better that than those bloodsuckers at the bank.

In truth, I don't believe that this rationale—or any of the nine others I've listed—truly reflects the fundamental reason why people play with The Stupid Free Parking Rule. There's another, *real* reason. And here it is.

10. We do not care if it makes the game worse— we are not interested in a good game.

I know that sounds mean, but hear me out. Nobody wants to watch *Schindler's List* or *Moonlight* every time they go to the movies. There is a time and a place for brilliantly written, beautifully shot, hauntingly performed masterpieces of cinematic art that move you to tears and challenge you to re-think your most fundamental ideas about the human condition. For most people, that time is not every single visit to a movie theatre.

The thing about a boilerplate blockbuster like *Revenge of the Mega-Transformitrons XVII* is that you know exactly what you are going to get—like ordering a Big Mac for dinner. It might not be very good, but it will be mediocre in exactly the way you expect. If you can understand dining and movie-going decisions like that, you can understand the reason for the popularity of *Monopoly*, and perhaps even the Stupid Free Parking Rule.

And this is where I part company with my fellow game snobs. If you are interested in the intricacies of game design and whether or not a game's rules are any "good," you need to understand that you are not the target audience for *Monopoly*. The Stupid Free Parking Rule serves its purpose by satisfying—if not necessarily *entertaining*—that audience, and it will continue doing so no matter how much it bothers people like us.

Not all art and entertainment is intended for the same people, and the ones outside a mass-market target audience often express disdain and disapproval for those who lap it up. When people really love something you hate, something clearly not intended for you, you will probably find their love of it annoying. And the more passionate you are about that art form, the more intense that feeling will be. Film buffs despise Michael Bay's oeuvre and its box-office dominance, hard-core foodies loathe McDonalds and the sort of culinary style it represents, and serious readers are aghast at the popularity of Dan Brown. Yet all that loathing and superiority does not make these products less beloved by their fans. If anything, it gives them another reason to smile, knowing that snooty critics (and game snobs like me) are rolling their eyes and sometimes even gnashing their teeth.

Maybe you love games so much that you pull your hair out knowing there are adults out there un-ironically enjoying games like *Monopoly*. You need to remember that those players are not acting out of ignorance. They have not forgotten what playing *Monopoly* is actually like. They are playing because they know exactly what it is like and that is the experience they want. They might even dislike the same things about it as you do. They might get three or four hours in and say, "Will someone please bankrupt me soon so this can end?" That does not mean they would have a better experience playing by the rules as written or even playing a "better" game.

Let people play the way they want, my fellow game snobs, and do not give them a hard time for doing so. By all means, invite them to play your preferred games as well, and hold fast to the hope that they will enjoy those, too. Just remember that they will not learn to love the things we love through browbeating and condescension.

CHAPTER NINE

All Your Culture Are Belong To Us

(Jonathan Kay: Lessons from Rising Sun,
Puerto Rico, John Company, Legend of
the Five Rings)

IN EARLY 2017, Singapore-based game company CMON launched *Rising Sun*, one of the year's most successful titles. Conceived by Eric Lang, the company's own Canadian-born director of game design, *Rising Sun* is a big, ambitious heavily stylized strategy game in which players take on the role of clan leaders seeking to dominate a mythical rendition of feudal Japan, complete with activist deities (*kami* 神), wandering mercenaries (*rōnin* 浪人) and even other-worldly creatures (*yōkai*, 妖怪) that serve the clans as powerful combatants.

Thanks in large part to the attractive miniatures used to represent combatants and the stunning map of Japan that comprises the board, *Rising Sun* became an instant hit from the moment CMON made copies of the game available on Kickstarter. Demand only swelled when gamers were informed that the first cohort of Kickstarter customers would get special features, including a bonus *yōkai* known as the *Kotahi*, a tall, angular, menacing-looking figure with a long staff and crown of fire. When I first played *Rising Sun* at a convention in Toronto, the game was the talk of the room. I ordered my own copy online that day.

A few months later, on the evening of January 21, 2018, a user on the popular website BoardGameGeek (BGG) posted an inquiry about *Rising Sun*. "As I checked the Monsters, I wonder where 'Kōtahi' comes from," he wrote. "I'm actually a Japanese but never heard of it. Does it come from another Asian country, or is it an original monster made by CMON?" The user, Yoshiya Shindo, noted that the name of the monster would appear to translate as "elder metal"—a weird way to describe a powerful supernatural apparition.

That same evening, the hive mind of BGG went to work with users noting that they could find only one on-point reference to the term *Kōtahi* associated with Japanese monster lore—and that was a garbled entry on the Wikipedia page "List of legendary creatures from Japan." It defined the creature as a "Manawa Bradford, a spirit monkey that is very hairy and gets engulfed in rage." A Google search for "Manawa Bradford" yielded only one seemingly relevant hit—the Facebook page of a New Zealand board gamer named Kotahi-Manawa Bradford. When an enterprising blogger reached out to Mr. Bradford, Bradford politely explained that he was not a Japanese monster but that he did have a reputation for being "engulfed in rage" when the dice failed him. The Wikipedia entry for *Kōtahi* appears to have been an in-joke with his friends, one of whom made the edit on the site. "Prior to my reaching out," the blogger reported, Mr. Bradford "was unaware of the existence of *Rising Sun* or his presence in the game."

CMON responded to the discovery with a light-hearted announcement to the effect that Mr. Bradford would be getting a free copy of the game in honor of his unwitting contribution. The *Kōtahi* figurine, however, did not appear in copies of *Rising Sun* shipped after the Kickstarter rollout, upsetting some members of the board game community. "So is this going to change anything?" asked one angry user on the popular *Shut Up & Sit Down* gaming site. "Ignorantly using a culture for game design without consulting or partnering with a person from that culture has been criticized yet remains common. Maybe some designers think cultural appropriation is too intangible an idea to cause a change in approach, but here is a practical example that is causing real embarrassment for a game company."

As for Kotahi-Manawa Bradford, a resident of the small New Zealand town of Dannevirke, he briefly became a minor celebrity. "This is the most exciting thing to happen in Dannevirke since someone tried to open a brothel there in 2008," declared a local. "It lasted precisely three weeks."

* * *

The concept of cultural appropriation has been around, in some form, for decades. The work of Columbia University scholar Edward Said—author of the 1978 book *Orientalism*—was especially influential in this regard. Said argued that western depictions of eastern cultures rely on crude, sentimental, and demeaning stereotypes, and his concerns spread from university liberal-arts curricula to mainstream culture, especially on social media where Twitter mobs often descend on ordinary people who post pictures of themselves in sombreros or kimonos.

In 2018, when an eighteen-year-old Salt Lake City teenager wore a traditional Chinese *qipao* dress to her grad, a Twitter user named Jeremy Lam (@jere_bare) called her out with the line "My culture is NOT your goddamn prom dress." That tweet received tens of thousands of likes. But the target, Keziah Daum, did not back down, declaring: "To everyone causing so much negativity: I mean no disrespect to the Chinese culture. I'm simply showing my appreciation to their culture. I'm not deleting my post because I've done nothing but show my love for the culture. It's a fucking dress. And it's beautiful."

While the underlying subject (prom attire) was trivial, the incident reflected the ongoing debate about cultural appropriation, whether the alleged appropriation is contained in film, literature, clothing, or board gaming: you're-stealing-my-culture vs. relax-it's-an-inanimate object. In some cases, these controversies have spilled out of the online world and caused real-world consequences. At Yale in 2015, a professor's email suggesting that students did not need to be lectured about appropriative Halloween costumes caused a campus-wide tempest that ended with her being hounded out of the university. And in recent years, whole novels have been unpublished (especially in the young adult genre) because of accusations that the author has misunderstood this or that culture.

As my co-author Joan notes in her chapter on *Cards Against Humanity*, there have been some controversies of this type in the board-gaming world. And Canada's biggest gaming convention now has rules that prohibit "anti-feminism" on the gaming floor, and has pledged itself to "celebrate all races, ethnicities, body-types, the full spectrum of genders, all sexual identities, and persons with a range of abilities and ability challenges." But that said, the board gaming subculture, as of this writing, has not witnessed anything comparable to, say, the Gamergate controversy that rocked video gamers. Even Eric Lang faced little backlash over the *Kōtahi* episode, which made news on gaming blogs but otherwise does not seem to have hurt the designer or his company.

The same is true of *Teotihuacan: City of Gods*, a 2018 strategy game with an ancient Mesoamerica theme, published by NSKN. The game's original promotional materials read: "Travel back in time thousands of years to the greatest city of the Aztecs. Witness the glory and the twilight of the powerful pre-Columbian civilization. Strategize, accrue wealth, gain the favor of the gods, and become the builder of the magnificent Pyramid of the Sun." But as critics noted, Teotihuacan was not an Aztec city. It had been built by a predecessor civilization and was occupied by the Aztecs as a ruin. Indeed, Aztec society did not even manifest itself until the fourteenth century. A time-traveling board gamer going back in time "thousands of years" would have overshot the mark substantially. Worse, the competitive premise of the game, which required players to develop Teotihuacan before the Europeans showed up, suggests the designers confused Teotihuacan with Tenochtitlan, which was the actual Aztec capital and sat fifty kilometers away.

The chastened designers cleaned things up in the final product which now, more vaguely, invites players to "travel back in time to the greatest city in Mesoamerica." And instead of awaiting the arrival of the Spaniards, players now compete in anticipation of "the dawn of the Aztecs." But even if the game's very title no longer butchers the historical record, the game's on-the-fly re-branding suggests a rushed attempt to avoid criticism (and also shows how flimsy the historical premise was to the game's actual mechanics, which are unchanged). And given the cultural climate we now inhabit, it made me wonder why such episodes have not generated more backlash within the board-gaming subculture.

One common theme that came up when I asked fellow board gamers about this was the power dynamic that exists between the alleged appropriator and the appropriated culture. At the height of Daum's mobbing, social media users from China tweeted their support for her, telling Twitter that they were delighted to see an American girl enjoying fashions inspired by their own rich history. China has a population of almost 1.4 billion people, a rich and well-documented history, and a thriving culture. No one in China is worried that a prom dress will undermine or distort China's collective self-image. The same is true of Japanese people in regard to *Rising Sun* and similar Japanese-themed board games. Shortly after the news about the game's bogus *Kōtahi* monster emerged, I spoke to Japanese board game journalist Mihoko Terasaki about whether this aroused concerns about cultural appropriation in Japan—another large Asian country with its own richly defined historical identity. Her response was that the whole idea of "cultural appropriation" is not really controversial in Japan because its whole thriving modern culture is based on the adaptation of influences from outsiders. And if anything, Japan needed more, not less, cultural mixing: "We seldom have enough support for those who take on the challenge of new ideas." She was unsure how to translate "cultural appropriation" into her own language. She called it *pakuri-bunka*, which might be translated as "plagiarism culture," or less charitably, "rip-off culture." Which is to say, she saw the only real issue as being whether the "appropriation" is so severe as to constitute full-blown copyright infringement: "If someone is a true creator of an original idea, then it wouldn't be unreasonable for them to get angry [at a plagiarist]."

* * *

The idea of cultural appropriation often gets lumped in with the larger notion of "political correctness" but the two concepts are distinct. While allegations of cultural appropriation can relate to alleged acts of coopting other cultures in an *appreciative* manner, allegations of political correctness typically target the opposite type of behavior in which a speaker, writer, or artist treats another people or culture in crude, objectifying, or insulting terms. The examples of *Teotihuacan: City of Gods* and *Rising Sun* show how these two categories can overlap. In both cases, the designers presented their work as a sort of homage to an ancient civilization and then produced games that betrayed the shallowness of their research, opening themselves to accusations that they were exploiting another culture for a quick buck.

Another, separate kind of controversy can develop when a designer creates a game whose premise is roughly true to a historical record steeped in racist predation and slaughter. In a 2018 article entitled "Representations of Colonialism in Three Popular, Modern Board Games," authors Cornel Borit, Melania Borit and Petter Olsen note that colonial exploration and development is a hugely popular theme in modern board games because it aligns with the modern preference for games that present players with the chance to build up a civilization turn by turn. Even *Catan* can be seen as a colonial game: players are cast as clan leaders invading a fictional *terra nullius* that, in real life, one would expect to be inhabited by indigenous peoples. In 2019, a group of Canadian gamers tried to do something about this, hosting a "Decolonization Game Jam" in Brantford, Ont., with the goal of "deconstructing and reconstructing . . . games such as *Settlers of Catan* and *Small World*, rewriting their rules to decolonize the games and in so doing encourage equitable, sustainable, and respectful behaviours towards other players, peoples, and lands."

The focus of the event was "so-called 3x and 4x games—built around the pillars of exploration, expansion, exploitation, and extermination." And it is quite true that various popular games in this category invoke some fairly dark historical themes. In the above-referenced 2009 game *Small World*, for instance, fantastical creatures within a fictional landmass must extinguish helpless "lost tribes" en route to military confrontation with one another. Similarly, in the epic space opera *Twilight Imperium* (1997), players are tasked with conquering whole planets, essentially putting themselves in the boots of Darth Vader.

One of the case studies in the above-referenced "Representations of Colonialism" is the popular 2002 strategy game *Puerto Rico*, in which players take on the role of Spaniards newly arrived on the island of—you guessed it—Puerto Rico, all seeking to create plantations and extract as much indigo, sugar, tobacco and coffee as possible to ship back to the European homeland. To get ahead, the authors note, each player "needs a number of the small black discs that come into the game each round. In the game rules, these are referred to as 'colonists,' but in practice and from the historical background, it is clear that these discs represent slaves. In addition, there are no mechanisms in the game for slowing down growth or penalties for extracting resources too quickly or using 'colonists' too intensively. There are numerous exchanges in various discussion forums pointing out how politically incorrect the game is, and some players feel uncomfortable with the game for this reason." Nevertheless, the game is ranked in the top fifteen worldwide.

The existence of these themes in popular board games can produce surreal scenes. We live in an age when, among the progressive subcultures of arts, academia, and activism, a person can lose her job or friends merely by liking or retweeting a controversial pundit. Yet at avowedly "inclusive" board game conventions, where the crowd is largely cut from the same highly progressive political cloth, one routinely sees diverse sets of people (including me) playing games such as *Puerto Rico* or *Small World* with nary a concern about the somewhat horrifying historical premises at play.

Even amidst my personal circle of friends, I see this pattern. During a recent playing of the American railroad-building game *1830: Railways & Robber Barons*, one of the players casually noted that the most profitable rail line on the map-board was, in historical terms, likely transporting slaves up and down the southern part of America's Atlantic coast. We paused to ponder this for a moment but went right on playing despite the fact that all of the people I saw seated around the table were social liberals, deeply committed to diversity and inclusion in all aspects of their real lives.

How to explain this seeming paradox? The simplest explanation is that a fun game is a fun game, and even the most committed social justice champion is going to think twice before swearing off a game she loves. While there is not much personal cost to railing against a book author you are supposed to dislike (since you can always secretly read their books in private), a serious board gamer is going to need to think twice before making similar grand gestures, since gaming is a *social* act. To the extent she goes public with her concerns about a game on Twitter or Facebook, she will be pre-empted from playing the game again without looking like a hypocrite in front of other players. The stakes, in other words, are higher.

It also might be the case of fearing the slippery slope. Once you interrogate the premise of one game, you will feel intellectually obligated to interrogate all of them. *Monopoly* is about Depression-era real-estate predation. *Battleship* is about sending sailors to watery graves. *Operation* is about killing a helpless patient in a hospital. The act of playing games requires a firm grasp of the bright line that separates reality from make-believe. And once that line breaks down, board gaming becomes impossible. As the experience of many authors shows, well-intentioned but arguably overwrought concerns about cultural appropriation already threaten to draw boundaries around the imagination of authors and artists and it would deeply regrettable if the same were to constrain the imagination of game designers.

There is also the issue of political and cultural context. One of the reasons Gamergate became such a flashpoint for women who felt shoved out of male-dominated video game culture is that this world truly was saturated by genuinely toxic male behavior. As a fan of first-person-shooter video games going back to the 1980s, I can attest that online taunts always quickly degenerated to the crudest forms of homophobia, sexism, and racism—something I have never observed in board gaming, which involves more thought and less adrenaline. As the recent explosion in female video gaming shows, there was a pent-up demand for a gaming culture (including more inclusive game titles) that served women and men alike. At the same time, the demands for female inclusion in the digital world more

Back in 1997, the production values of this Third Edition copy of *Catan* were considered rather impressive.

Can you spot the illegal moves, *Scrabble* fans?

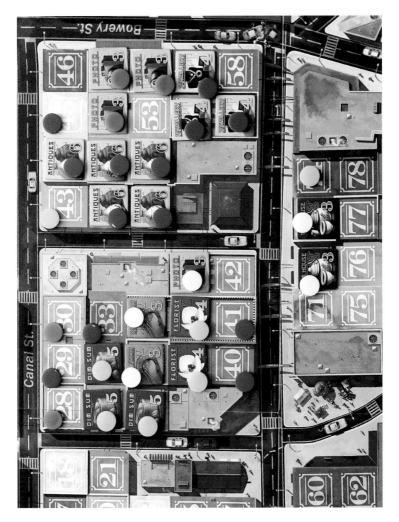

In this part of *Chinatown*, the red player wants to extend that antiques shop into block 43. How much can its owner get away with charging?

The ground-breaking *Pandemic Legacy*.

The hordes of undead in *Dead of Winter* are limitless. No matter how many you kill, there always seem to be more of them rising up.

Nothing happens when you land on this space in *Monopoly* . . . officially, at least.

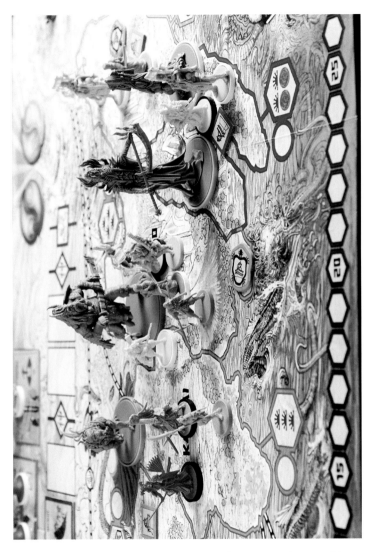

The beautiful and mythologically questionable miniature figures of *Rising Sun*.

A small sample of the resources that can help you survive in *Greenland*.

The surprisingly diabolical game of *Scattergories*.

After a promising start for this round of *Telestrations*, the game threatens to get boring when "Queen" becomes too easy a picture to draw and identify.

May 17, 1940: German troops assault the Belgian town of Kapelle-op-den-Bos in a game of *Advanced Squad Leader*.

"For me," says Joan Moriarity, "this book was a gateway into a larger world."

generally ran headlong into male complaints that politically correct culture was invading one of their last remaining bro treehouses. Gamergate was just the match that lit all this tinder aflame.

The world of board gaming, I would argue, has no equivalent "tinder." As noted in the second chapter of this book, the modern board-gaming renaissance came of age in the 1990s among a group of people—mostly young, college-educated urbanites—who already had the cultural training required to develop self-awareness about how their behaviors could affect their female, visible minority and LGBT friends. There is more social trust among players, and less need to turn every flare up into a Gamergate-style existential battle for the soul of their hobby.

Finally, as has been widely noted, many people simply act *stupider* online than they do when, say, assembled around a card table in someone's real-life living room. Modern video games allow dozens of players to compete simultaneously in massively networked gaming forums, with their characters hopping around the same arenas; as each increasingly inane screen chat and voiceover is broadcast to all, every troll who wants to provoke everyone else into a flame war is thereby provided a large audience. Thankfully, this has no equivalent in the world of board gaming. In gaming, as in other cultures, the medium truly does affect the message.

* * *

One of the most interesting board-gaming experiences I ever had was in 2016 when I was visiting a Tuesday-night gaming salon in New York City hosted by the legendary J.R. Tracy, a former hedge fund manager who has purchased an entire Chelsea condominium just to house his board games. On the night I visited, he had all eleven attendees assemble around a table for a round of *Secret Hitler*, an intriguing but bizarre team-based game in which players are secretly assigned the role of either liberal or fascist during the last months of the Weimar Republic, with the liberals' objective being to assassinate the fascist who has been randomly tagged as Hitler. In the end, my liberals lost when the Führer stepped forward in the real-life form of Horst, a German friend of J.R.'s who, as it happened, had recently moved to New York from Berlin. "This is kind of an uncomfortable situation," he said in his decidedly German-accented English. In another room, this sort of thing might have been genuinely awkward. But in this room full of seasoned gamers, it sent all of us, including Horst, into a lengthy spasm of laughter. Real Nazis are terrifying and evil. Game Nazis are funny.

In a concluding section of "Representations of Colonialism," the authors worry about the political damage that games such as *Puerto Rico* can inflict on the collective psyche. "Trapped into playing the stereotyped colonist, the player can never experience the world through the eyes of the Other," they write. "We wonder whether the virtual experience of participating in the colonial history that such games produce could possibly encourage players to exhibit the behavior and attitude of colonizers."

I disagree. While it is hard to prove or disprove such a proposition without a controlled experiment, my own experience is that a psychologically healthy person does not intermingle the politics of *Puerto Rico* with the historical politics of Puerto Rico.

That is not to say that board games cannot teach players about real-life history or, at least, inspire them to learn. Indeed, I provide a concrete example of this in my next chapter. But the use of colonial themes may actually have a positive impact because it can help a post-colonial observer understand how supposedly civilized societies could impose the evil of colonialism on other peoples with, as they believed, a clean conscience. As Hannah Arendt taught us, evil does not always announce itself with cackling laughter and a black heart worn on one's sleeve.

Consider the 2017 Sierra Madre game *John Company*, in which players take the role of ambitious British businessmen and socialites operating within dynastic factions of the British East India Company. On the surface, the game answers to many of the criticisms that might be hurled at *Puerto Rico*. The protagonists are colonialists and the colonized people of India fade into the background as players squabble over the trade spoils of subjugated Indian regions before returning to London with their loot. Hardly an edifying premise.

Yet to play the game is also to educate oneself about the mind of a colonizer. Within the first few turns, one becomes enmeshed in the company's cutthroat power politics, with the actual geographic and demographic reality of India fading into the background. As was typical among real colonialists and their corporate affiliates, operatives within the British East India Company did not set out to be evil and rapacious. The exploitation of India was embedded in its system of economic incentives. While playing *John Company* is no substitute for real education about British involvement in the Indian subcontinent during the Victorian era, it at least shows a player how evil can be bred from amoral greed, a lesson that arguably applies to the excesses of our own capitalist system in certain contexts.

* * *

Does this mean that sensitivity should never intrude into the world of board games or, by extension, other creative subcultures? The answer is no. Much as we all love to rail against political correctness, there are some instances in which content decisions really should be made with a view to the emotional effect on community members. In general, however, the case for sensitivity—call it political correctness if you will—is strongest when the targeted behavior exists on the real-life side of the life-art divide.

Here's one final game example: *Legend of the Five Rings,* a collect-ible card game originally created by Alderac Entertainment Group in 1995. While the game is not as famous as the somewhat simi-lar *Magic: The Gathering,* it has some comparable mechanics and a devoted cult following that cheered mightily when the game was recently reissued in revised form after being discontinued in 2015.

The fantasy world in which *Legend of the Five Rings* takes place is Rokugan, a fictional place resembling feudal Japan. Much of the game's campy East Asia atmospherics are borrowed from Japanese game and media culture. And here is where the new publishers of *Legend of the Five Rings,* Fantasy Flight Games, got into trouble.

"The game was originally developed in the 1980s when people were first bringing in Asian products because they thought it was cool," says Malaysian writer Calvin Wong Tze Loon, a leading critic of cultural appropriation in board games. "A lot of it didn't age well. For a long time, there was a tradition that before every sanctioned [*Legend of the Five Rings*] tournament, there would be a chant. It was like something you would do before a sports game, and it might have seemed harmless. But it wasn't."

The specific Japanese chant had a call-and-response format, with the tournament director yelling "*Utsu!*" and the players yelling "*Banzai!*" Taken together, the meaning is idiomatically equivalent to "Let's do this!" But as Wong points out, *banzai* was the term shouted by Japanese infantrymen before conducting attacks against their enemies during World War II and earlier regional campaigns.

"When the card game was rebooted by Fantasy Flight, they brought back the chant," Wong tells me. "When I heard it, I saw that a lot of people were super-emotional. They were *happy* that the chant was back. I was like, ;you can't use the term *banzai.*' [In Malaysia], the Japanese rounded up people who looked like me, changed our names, put us into Japanese schools. I have relatives who lived through that war. They're still alive. I told all this to

Fantasy Flight, and [in 2017] they changed the chant to 'For Honor, For Glory.' To their credit, they realized that what they had done was causing harm."

Did Fantasy Flight do the right thing? Depends on who you ask. On the *Legend of the Five Rings* message boards, Japanese-speaking fans pointed out that there are plenty of contexts in which *banzai* is used without any militaristic meaning whatsoever. Others countered that the combat theme of the card game gave a very specific, and ominous, overtone to the gesture. As with all internet arguments, this one got nasty and ended inconclusively. Whatever the merits of the arguments, the point is that the company was concerning itself with the real actions of real people attending real company-organized tournaments, not the abstract symbols or words contained within the pretend universe of the game. As human beings, we subject ourselves to all sorts of restrictions on our real-world behavior. It is one of the reasons we seek out imaginary domains where our minds and meeples must run free.

CHAPTER TEN

Inside the Mind of an Inuit Hero

(Jonathan Kay: Lessons from Greenland, *and* 1812: The Invasion of Canada)

A BOWHEAD WHALE IS A majestic and intimidating creature, up to sixty feet in length, weighing up to one hundred tons, with a triangular hunk of bone for a skull that the bowhead uses to smash through Arctic ice on its way to the ocean surface. Amazingly, the Indigenous peoples of northern Europe and North America found a way to kill and harvest these massive creatures without modern ships or weapons. Their hunts, conducted by small kin groups operating out of coastal hunting camps, carried extraordinarily risk. The enterprise was nevertheless worthwhile because a single bowhead might provide enough food and fuel to keep the hunters and their families alive for a year.

Any visitor to the Far North will marvel at how a human community can survive, and even thrive in a region where almost any modern human would almost immediately die of exposure or starvation. That the Inuit were up to this challenge year after year, generation after generation, is a testament to their discipline and ingenuity as hunters, and as inventors and field engineers, notwithstanding the sentimental "noble savage" stereotypes that still persist. One of the great frustrations of whalers everywhere, for instance, was the tendency of spears to detach from a whale (or seal, or walrus) as it submerged. The Thule (the proto-Inuit ancestors of the modern Inuit) solved this problem with an ingenious device known as a toggling harpoon. The weapon featured a spear point divided in two parts, connected by sinew, with one part acting as a cap to the other. When a beast was impaled, the spear point's cap would detach from the main shaft and penetrate the beast's blubber and muscle—rotating as it traveled, so that when the hunter pulled the spear back toward his boat, the cap would hold fast within the whale, like a corkscrew in the neck of a wine bottle, allowing the carcass to be pulled back to shore.

No one taught me such skills while I was growing up in Canada, largely because no one ever taught me much of *anything* about Indigenous peoples. Before the 1990s, which brought with it a revolution in the way First Nations, Inuit, Innu and Métis people fought for their political rights and raised awareness of their history, Indigenous peoples were largely invisible to most non-Indigenous Canadians. Thankfully, all that has changed, as the extensive coverage of Indigenous themes on my daughters' public school curricula clearly shows. Unfortunately, I am yet to see evidence that these materials are truly seizing students' imagination.

Perhaps the most popular text now used to educate young Canadian children about the country's Indigenous peoples is *The Secret Path*, an illustrated book about Chanie Wenjack (1954-1966), an Anishinaabe boy who fled a residential school in Ontario and subsequently died from hunger and exposure. The story is tragic and haunting. An accumulation of narratives of this sort can have a numbing effect on one's imagination, much like the Holocaust-education materials I learned when I went to Jewish school. Even the worst tales of cruelty can become repetitive.

Today's children are discouraged from playing racist schoolyard games such as "cowboys and Indians," since they portray Indians as savages and proto-terrorists. That is a welcome development, although those racist games at least presented Indigenous peoples as having some form of agency. A model of representation that centers entirely on victimization can strip Indigenous people of any agency whatsoever. This is not only condescending and ahistorical but also serves to discourage non-Indigenous people from exploring the fascinating histories of Indigenous peoples.

Harold Johnson, a Cree writer from Treaty 6 territory in northern Saskatchewan, wrote about manufactured passivity in his 2016 book *Firewater*, wherein he described how the appearance of the *kiciwamanawak*—white people who brought Christianity, capitalism, alcohol, disease and the ravages of colonialism—created a false narrative about "the dirty, lazy, drunken Indian." They eclipsed what Johnson called "our own stories about ourselves wherein we were the heroes. We were great hunters, providers, even warriors when need be. We were wise grandmothers and medicine people. We told stories about ourselves and about *mithosin kitaskinâw*— our beautiful land." One of the effects of Europe's colonization of the Americas was that many of the old stories were, quite literally, destroyed.

This theft of Indigenous agency has itself become embedded as a meta-theme in modern Indigenous folklore. Johnson opened his 2016 book with the tale of a legendary Cree hero named Wîsahkicâhk watching television: "And he saw an Indian story on there. But the story didn't seem right. It was all mixed up. He went to check the original. He had it somewhere. The Creator gave Wîsahkicâhk a whole bag of stories back at the beginning of time and he told Wîsahkicâhk, 'Here, look after these, the people are going to need them to know how to live a good life, and they are going to need them when things get difficult.' But Wîsahkicâhk couldn't find them. Man, he was in trouble now. He lost the stories the Creator gave him."

As a white writer, I have no expertise or moral authority in regard to the complex project by which Wîsahkicâhk and his counterparts in other Indigenous communities will get his stories back. I can, however, speak to the process by which today's white intellectuals have, often with good intentions, systematically undermined that rehabilitation project. While Indigenous peoples were, as Johnson writes, "hunters, providers, even warriors," they are often transformed by today's white writers and activists into a collective of endlessly suffering Chanie Wenjacks, baby Christs for our secular age. Or they are portrayed as elves of the forest, preternaturally wise Lorax-type figures who are trotted out as political props for the convenience of white environmentalists. Chanie's suffering was real, as was the suffering of the thousands of other innocents who suffered similar fates. These stories can inspire guilt and pity among school students, yet they are not representative of ancient civilizations whose extraordinary accomplishments have the power to fascinate and inspire.

* * *

Board game designer Philipp Klarmann might seem not seem like the sort of creative genius likely to blaze a new trail in the field of Indigenous education. He is as white as me and from Germany, a country with no Indigenous population whatsoever. His other gaming credits include *Reichshoffen 1870*, a 2007 game about the Franco-Prussian War, and *Magenta 1859*, a similarly obscure offering about the Second Italian War of Independence. *Greenland*, a game he conceived in 2014, has attracted far more notice.

Klarmann has no apparent personal connection to any Indigenous community anywhere. In an interview with Geof Gambill of *The*

Long View podcast, he said that the idea for *Greenland* popped into his head after reading a magazine article discussing various theories as to why Norse settlements vanished from Greenland in the fifteenth century, as well as a 2005 novel by Jane Smiley called *The Greenlanders*.

Modern Greenland—the continent not the game—is one of the least traveled places on earth. Now home to just fifty-six thousand people (almost all of whom inhabit Greenland's ice-free coast), the place now exists as an autonomous constituent of Denmark. A thousand years ago, however, the island witnessed an important historical saga that changed the fate of three different civilizations.

The plot of *Greenland*, the game, begins in the eleventh century as a tooth-and-claw struggle involving Norsemen, Inuit, and Tunit (an ancient, now extinct ice-fishing people, often described as Dorset). "Two centuries after the outlaw Erik the Red had misnamed this treeless ice-covered island *Grænland*, ten emaciated Norsemen clambered out of a rowboat and onto the pack ice," is how the preamble introduces the game. "It was the May after the hardest winter they could remember, and months earlier they had run out of stored food and hay. The clubsmen expected to harvest the first available meat of the year, doe-eyed harp seal pups abandoned on the ice. But they found only a volley of Thule arrows. The Skrælings [a disparaging Viking word for both the Thule and Tunit tribes] have superior numbers and Arctic survival skills. And if the Thule kill off the Norse and Tunit, they will rule Greenland alone."

In a 2014 interview, Klarmann's co-creator, Phil Eklund, set out the stunning back story of this inter-civilizational meeting on Greenland's shores. All three of these groups—Norse, Thule and Tunit—had originated tens of thousands of years previously within the same cluster of central Asian peoples. The Norse were part of the group that had migrated west to become northern Europeans. The Thule and Tinut were part of the group that migrated across the Bering Strait as Amerindians. About a thousand years ago, all three civilizations ran up against each other on the world's largest island, a sort of unintended reunion after thousands of years of separation.

Like other titles discussed in this book, *Greenland* is not a true "board game" because there is no real board. (An actual map of Greenland would have made little sense as a basis for gameplay, since the vast inland bulk of the island is uninhabitable.) During the imagined time frame of the game, just as now, Greenland was a marginal place for human habitation. Crops were difficult to grow and many of the tastiest animals also happened to be ferocious. (The name "Greenland" originated with what was, in effect, a cynical Norse marketing ploy aimed at attracting colonists to a land of supposed plenty.) Wood was so scarce on Greenland that ships traveled all the way to Labrador for imports. For their iron, Greenland's Indigenous metallurgists were restricted to bog deposits and the remains of a fifty-eight-ton iron-rich meteorite that hit northwest Greenland ten thousand years ago. Tools and weapons often had to be carved from whale bones and other exotic materials. The difference between life and death for many clans could be a single metal cooking pot passed along from mother to daughter, a critical tool to pasteurize the milk of domesticated livestock.

Competition in *Greenland* takes place through the struggle for resources, especially food, which can be won through the allocation of population tokens that represent each player's available hunters. There is some combat but most casualties are caused by hunting accidents and catastrophic climate shifts. Disease also plays a huge role. During my first game of *Greenland*, I established a strong lead over the other two players before an epidemic ravaged my seal-hunting camp, cutting my workforce in half. My Tunit and Norse opponents had meanwhile diversified by sending off colonizing forces to the "New World" of Vinland and Markland—known today as Canada—where, although potentially more dangerous than Greenland, rich bounties in metal and ivory could be had.

Each *Greenland* game turn, representing a generation of clan life, is full of existential choices. Elders can become whaling chiefs, warriors, trackers, mariners, or shamans. If food is scarce, an elder also can make a long final walk into the snow, so that his share of the food supply might be used to keep younger clansmen alive. If conditions are desperate and there are no ringed seal or (relatively) docile muskox to be had, the clan might risk hunting polar bears or orca. Walrus offer an especially rich bounty in food, blubber, and ivory but also can be driven into extinction. As the game progresses, new cataclysms and opportunities emerge. Players have the chance to cling to polytheism or embrace Christianity, marry the daughters of other players' chiefs, and even proselytize other players or prosecute heretics within their own society.

To win at *Greenland*, you do not just have to make careful decisions about what to hunt but also what technology to pursue. While the reductive nature of white entertainment culture tends to present northern peoples as timeless sages, the need to survive in this harsh climate sparked all sorts of extraordinary technological advances including dog sleds, slit-designed snow goggles, and the aforementioned toggle-headed harpoon (a technology that Europeans did not fully adapt until centuries later). Everyone has heard of the kayak. Fewer know the *umiak*, a much larger boat that could accommodate large families and more than a dozen oarsmen. The Thule made sails out of seal intestines. They even used some of their scarce wood to provide hunters and mariners with carved maps of Greenland's complex system of fjords and ice-sheets. Indeed, the advanced technologies that the Thule brought with them when they sent their whalers and war parties south and east out of Alaska help explain why, when the real battle for Greenland ended more than five centuries ago, the Inuit came out on top while the Norse fled and the Tunit passed into history.

Because *Greenland* is a game, it emphasizes the kinetic aspects of Indigenous societies: the sailing craft, the hunting techniques, the migrations. This presents a welcome contrast from the gauzy treatment that the Inuit tend to get in modern art, scholarship, and journalism which tends to lionize the Inuit on the basis of qualities (real or imagined) that (by no coincidence) are prized in modern academic culture: feminism, environmentalism, pacifism, and egalitarianism.

Klarmann, by his own admission, almost committed the opposite sin when he created the first draft of *Greenland*, turning the subject of Greenland history into a sort of tabletop version of "cowboys and Indians." "The first iteration only had the Vikings [Norse] in the game," he said in 2014. It was "a survival game where the Vikings start by expanding in the first part of the game, building a colony, and then thrive, and create a second or third, and then in the last part of the game you get *crushed*. The problem was, 'How do you make that interesting as an overarching storyline?'"

As I listened to the interview, I waited for Klarmann to talk about how he had an epiphany—how he had come to understand his own Eurocentrism, and that he was Othering the Tunit and Thule by stripping them of agency. Over a two-hour interview, however, he never mentioned any of this. He simply wanted to make a better game, which meant giving an inner life to the other societies that shared Greenland's land mass during the period depicted by the game.

Without intending to, Klarmann made the Indigenous players the game's real historical stars. While we all know that medieval Europeans had metal pots and swords, few first-time *Greenland* players will know that Indigenous hunters used a remarkable device called a seal scratcher to simulate the sound of a ringed seal clawing its way through an ice sheet, thereby signaling to other seals that the coast was clear. *Greenland* is full of marvelous little discoveries like this.

I am hardly the first writer to note the need to emphasize the agency of Indigenous peoples amidst the current surfeit of victim narratives, and one now often sees Indigenous themes and characters featured prominently in historical documentaries and novels. Nevertheless, it is hard for even the most creative artist to inspire people on a made-to-order basis. In 2018, for instance, famed Canadian musician-turned-politician Wab Kinew and illustrator Joe Morse produced a beautiful children's book called *Go Show The World: A Celebration of Indigenous Heroes*. It is a beautifully produced work, honoring such diverse figures as Shoeshone explorer Sacagawea, Olympian Jim Thorpe, Dr. Susan Laflesche Picotte, the great warrior Tecumseh, and NHL goalie Carey Price. Yet even in the way they announce themselves, such projects tend to have an unavoidably didactic quality to them.

Moreover, in life as in literature, the ability of a true hero to inspire will always be connected in her magnetism as a *singular* entity, her ability to bend people and events to her own intellect, courage, or will. A hero who is described as a mere component of a larger catalog is always deflated in the process, reduced to the status of educational prop.

I am trying to think how much less effective *Greenland* would be—both as a game, and as a tool for education—if it were instead called *Nunavut*, and were designed by, say, a committee of Canadian education officials seeking to create a tool to promote Indigenous/non-Indigenous reconciliation. Such a game would no doubt be run through so many focus groups and experts that it would come out the other side as a politically correct awareness-raising exercise with a few dice rolls thrown in. Which is not to say that raising awareness is a bad thing. It is not. But, as with falling in love and finding one's purpose in life, it tends to be something that happens when you are not trying to do it. Klarmann and Eklund did not care about getting players to admire Indigenous peoples, even if that is what they achieved. They were just two nerds trying to make a good game.

* * *

A good game, like a good movie or book, can put a player into the shoes of another human being. That is most obvious in a first person-style video game, where the action prompts a player to duck and wince as if she were experiencing the in-game action personally, becoming a hero of his own story. Tabletop games are more abstract but they can achieve an analogous result on a broader thematic scale.

To immerse oneself in *Greenland* is to inhabit the strategic and logistical challenges of the Norse, Thule or Tunit. (A subsequent game expansion also includes the Sámi, who were based in the northern part of Scandinavia although their connection to Greenland was, even by the designers' claims, somewhat speculative.) The connection a player feels with these ancient peoples does not come through pathos or empathy. For a competitive gamer who truly immerses herself in the game's historical premise, it is a naturally felt artifact that emerges from the inwardly felt heroism of role play. That is the way it was for me, certainly: catching whales, killing Norsemen, occupying Vinland—all of it brought me not just an endorphin rush but an enduring curiosity about Indigenous history, an effect that persisted well after the game was over.

Greenland is not an isolated example. I had a similar experience when I played the British side of the card-driven war game *1812: The Invasion of Canada*, in which I found myself commanding a mixed force of British Redcoats, militia, and Indigenous soldiers trying to fight off American invaders. While I had long known, in the abstract, that First Nations fighters had played a major role in the War of 1812, the game mechanics showed me exactly how well irregular Indigenous units—with their smaller logistical footprint and their ability to strike quickly across rivers and lakes— complimented the slower, heavier, regular British units.

I am not arguing that board games can lead Canada's Indigenous and non-Indigenous peoples to some sort of giant, collective kumbaya moment. I do think that my experiences with *Greenland* and *1812* supply a lesson that can be generalized to other media. One of the themes that have animated the rise of modern identity politics more generally, and the campaign against cultural appropriation specifically, has been the idea that whites and members of minority groups inhabit mutually unintelligible milieus. The only way social justice can be achieved is if the dominant group (whites) simply absorb, and uncritically accept, the narrative of pain and dispossession supplied by less privileged groups.

This social justice approach may work for some. It will never work for all. Even putting aside questions of race and tribe, humans are not trusting creatures. In many cases, they require some viscerally felt signal from within, some transformative experience, that allows them to step out of themselves and inhabit, even for brief fragments of time, another identity. This is why we honor books such as *Uncle Tom's Cabin* and *Handmaid's Tale*, or films such as *Schindler's List* and *Philadelphia*, which embed important messages under cover of art. While *Greenland* does not aspire to high art, I would submit that it can have the same edifying effect on those who engage with it.

CHAPTER ELEVEN

Scattergories and Sacrilege

(Joan Moriarity: Lessons from Scattergories*)*

T O A CERTAIN PURITANICAL stripe of society, games always have been disreputable. In the Victorian era, dice were associated with ne'er do-wells hence, as noted earlier, the teetotum from Milton Bradley's *Checkered Game of Life*. In the 1980s, there was an intense moral panic surrounding *Dungeons & Dragons*. Pearl-clutching citizens condemned *D&D*, declaring it the cause of suicide, occult beliefs, and devil-worship among vulnerable youths (we'll get to how it warped my own impressionable young mind in a later chapter). More recently, video games such as *DOOM* and *Grand Theft Auto* took their turns in the moral-panic spotlight, as new cohorts of pearl-clutchers and like-minded politicians sought to protect us from pixelated blood and guts.

Do games encourage bad behavior? Many gamers would be annoyed that anyone would ask such a question, insisting that games and the real world lie in entirely different spheres and that those who claim otherwise are suffering from an inability to distinguish fantasy from reality. You may be surprised to hear that I will not be making such a claim. I know all too well that the real answer is "it depends on the game," and the ones to watch out for aren't the violent or prurient specimens you might expect. The real threat comes from purportedly lighthearted fare that destroys human relationships, disguised in the sinister pretense of wholesome family fun.

Some of you already know the kind of social damage *Scattergories* can do at a family gathering. Others may be blissfully unaware. Fair warning to the latter group: you may be shocked when the veil is lifted to reveal the horrible truth.

Consider the rules of *Scattergories*. A round of this game consists of two phases: first writing, then scoring. During the writing phase, each player receives an identical list of twelve categories, such as "household tasks" or "modes of transportation" or "romantic movies." Then a random letter from the alphabet is chosen by rolling a big twenty-sided die. Then the players are given two minutes to fill privately a list of twelve examples from those categories, all of which must begin with the chosen letter. So if the letter is D, the above categories could be filled by "dusting," "dirigible," and "*Die Hard.*"

Or could they? *Die Hard* is about a man traveling to visit his estranged wife and children for Christmas and hoping to earn back their love. It is also about pitched gun battles and large explosions. Does it count as a romantic movie? We'll come back to that later.

On the surface, this phase makes *Scattergories* seem an innocuous, if dreary, family game. It is often labeled a "party game" but that implies a party-like atmosphere. Gregarious fun, rollicking hijinks, that sort of thing. *Scattergories* is more like being stuck in detention with nothing to do but your homework. Players sit quietly with their papers and pens, writing without talking to each other, without interacting or even looking at each other. They might as well be doing their taxes. This part of *Scattergories* is a silent, joyless chore.

Then it gets much worse. The scoring phase might more properly be called the arguing phase, and here is where the real damage is done.

Players go down their list of categories, counting how many they were able to fill with an appropriate thing starting with the appropriate letter, scoring one point for each, unless somebody else gave the same answer for that category. So "dusting," "dirigible" and "*Die Hard*" are each worth one point so long as nobody else wrote those down. And so long as everyone agrees that *Die Hard* counts as a romantic movie. And here we discover the true nature of *Scattergories*.

Answers are subject to challenge. Any player who is displeased with an answer given by another player can put it to a vote. If a majority of players deem the answer unacceptable, no point is scored. The game is not like *Scrabble* where the validity of an answer can be tested by comparing it with an impartial, authoritative list (even one as dubious as the *Scrabble* dictionary, which you will hear about the next chapter). It is more like *American Idol*, where your opponents are all Simon Cowell. You could write "*Doctor Zhivago*" or "*Dirty Dancing*" and the other players could disallow it with a majority vote, reasoning that it is not a very good movie, or not truly romantic by their personal definition, or because you voted against their claim that Cheez Whiz is a "popular kind of cream" in the previous round.

This is the crux of the matter. *Scattergories* is not a game about words. It is not a game about thinking quickly. It is not about conversation and fun. It is about office politics, bullying, vengeance, and psychic torture. It is labeled on the box cover as suitable for ages 12 and up.

In *Dungeons & Dragons*, players are rewarded in their adventures for defeating villains, saving innocent lives, discovering ancient secrets, and generally acting like heroes. You can murder people for no reason in *D&D* if you want to, although, murder is a crime in most fictional jurisdictions within the imaginary world where those adventures take place, which means you will fall afoul of local law enforcement in addition to other inconveniences. But even if your characters exist in a *D&D* universe where crime sometimes pays, what happens within the game, stays within the game. You can do well at the game without having to hurt real people. Love them or hate them, these types of game encourage players to remain within the magic circle, maintaining the purity of play.

Now back to *Scattergories*. What kind of behavior does this game reward? Having a large vocabulary? Sure, provided nobody else at the table has an equally large vocabulary. Remember, an answer given by another player does not score. Being creative? Sure, provided nobody else is also being creative, for the same reason.

The one thing you can do in *Scattergories* to reliably ensure improved performance and higher scores relative to your opponents is to be good at challenging. How do you accomplish that? By making cogent, substantive points that appeal to your fellow players' logic and reason? Please. Modern-day elections are decided by appeals to fear and loathing. Voting in *Scattergories* is the same. Just as if you were running for public office, the only way to get really good at *Scattergories* is to become a horrifyingly inhuman engine of misery and suffering. In other words, the most effective way to play *Scattergories* is to harm your opponents in real life. The game encourages, indeed, demands that its players violate the magic circle. For this reason, *Scattergories* is not merely a bad game and unhealthy for your relationships. From my point of view, as someone who considers the play space sacred, it is sacrilegious.

How bad can it get? Let us put together a primer on how to master the game and we will see. Obviously, you cannot challenge every single answer. The other players will tire of you and vote you down as a matter of course. Instead, you need to challenge just enough of the answers given by your closest rivals to ensure you pull ahead of them in the score.

Which tactics work best? That depends on the individual. In general, players who dislike confrontation will be your easiest, most vulnerable targets, and the most profitable to exploit. If you know someone is willing to go along to get along, then you will not need to do much. A subtle threat that you will take it personally if they do not vote in your favor is often enough to bring them to heel. Sometimes an arched eyebrow will suffice. Players who have close emotional ties to you are also good targets because they are subject to emotional blackmail. They care about your feelings. Make sure they understand that your feelings will be deeply hurt if they do not take your side. If you are playing with family members who depend on you for various things, or friends who have accepted your help from time to time, you can remind them of everything you have done for them and imply that next time they need your help, you will remember their vote. You also know all the little things they have done over the years that shame or embarrass them. You know their weaknesses and fears.

There will usually be one or two players who are more intractable than others. No problem. You do not need everyone to vote in your favor, just the majority. Prey upon the weakest, pushing only as hard as you need to, and victory will be yours. If you lay it on too thick, the others might call you out. Press just hard enough, and no harder, and you can respond to any criticism with "Oh come on, it's just a game!"

Some people talk about "games ruining friendships." Usually, the game in question will be *Monopoly* or *Risk* or *Diplomacy*. Yet when a player in those games makes a choice that helps or harms another player, they typically do it out of self-interest. If you and another player make a deal not to attack each other for a few turns so you can both focus your attention on your other opponents, it serves both your interests within the game to do so. And if one of you has more to gain by suddenly and unceremoniously breaking the truce and stabbing the other in the back, then that too is understandable, because the betrayer has something to gain (more territory) and something to lose (the benefit of détente with a neighbor). The strategic and tactical considerations of these choices can be justified within the context of the game. You are all being bastards together, fairly and openly. The magic circle is unbroken.

In *Scattergories*, these considerations do not apply. Why should you vote in favor of "drapes" counting as "a household task?" Is there any way to obtain an objectively correct answer to this question? No. Will it affect your score either way? No. Favoritism is the only metric for what does or does not constitute an acceptable answer.

When deciding how to vote in *Scattergories,* your main consideration is how to appease players who might inflict emotional damage upon *you*. If you are lucky, there will be only one such player at your table. Everyone will gingerly step around such a player's ego and let them win. Of course, this will make them want to play again, and often. When the title of this game comes up in conversation and someone announces, "I love that game! I'm so good at it," believe their boasting and beware their company.

When there are two or more such players, it becomes a contest of who can be the subtlest in cruelty, who can inflict the most harm while appearing to be the most reasonable. Contests of this nature are the essence of painful family gatherings. With multiple manipulators to appease and no possible way of finding middle ground, the stage is set for the re-opening of old wounds, reminders of past misdeeds, revisiting of old political disagreements, and so on.

I am not innocent of bad behavior at the game table. I have lost my composure in a game twice in my adult life, and I am still ashamed of what I did, years after the fact. Everyone blasphemes from time to time, even the faithful. However, if it happens over and over because, as with *Scattergories*, this sort of behavior is fundamental to the game's design, and the game becomes a sacrilege.

It is also possible to play *Scattergories* without having to deal with all of this unpleasantness. If it were miserable for everyone, it would never have sold so well. If you play with a group of well-adjusted people who are less interested in winning than in spending a pleasant time together, you can contain it within the circle and keep faith with play. You can still spend half the game sitting silently doing your homework in detention, and the other half genuinely trying to figure out if "donkey" should count as a "mode of transportation," and it need not be hell on Earth. But there is no need to subject yourself to the risk. Many other party games will serve the same purpose, and better.

Take *Hive Mind* (2016), for example, designed by Richard Garfield and published by Calliope Games. It has the same "everyone writes a list of words and then we score points" premise but the writing time is much shorter and, crucially, you score based on matches with the other players, regardless of whether your answers are "correct." There is no need to argue about right and wrong unless you find the discussion interesting and fun (and, even then, it has no effect on who wins the game so it is a safe territory for conflict-free discussion). *Last Word* (2005) by Arthur Wagner, published by Buffalo Games, offers a louder, more gregarious approach by substituting yelling for writing. While arguments about what does or does not constitute a true answer can break out, the stakes are much lower for each individual word as far as the score is concerned, and the silly, frantic feel of the game lowers the emotional stakes to the point where far fewer players will be seduced by the lure of the darkness outside the circle.

We live in a polarized age. Emotions run high. Play should not contribute to making us hate each other. *Scattergories*, simply put, is the place where friendships go to die.

CHAPTER TWELVE

The Fine Line Between Work and Play

(Jonathan Kay: Lessons from Scrabble)

I N 2018, MERRIAM-WEBSTER released the sixth edition of its *Official Scrabble Players Dictionary*. Like previous versions, the new volume attracted attention. Newly playable words include *bestie* (a best friend), *zomboid* (resembling a zombie), *beatdown* (an overwhelming defeat), *ew* (used to express disgust), *frowny* (showing a frown), *qapik* (a monetary subunit in Azerbaijan) and—this one had the *Scrabble* community all abuzz—*OK*.

I love when tiny modifications to any game system attract wide attention but I have to admit that I dislike Scrabble and resent its high status within the genre. It is not that I dislike words or games that revolve around words. I love words. What I love about words, however, is their meaning and etymology which few real *Scrabble* players bother studying because such details are irrelevant to scoring. The *Scrabble* gaming system treats our rich English linguistic tapestry as a string of permissible codes. The game's only link to usage in the real world lies in the point values assigned to the various letter tiles, which U.S. inventor Alfred Butts based on how often the letters appeared in publications such as *The New York Times* in the 1930s. The rarer the letter the more points it brings, from ten points for Q and Z down to one point for the vowels and the most common consonants.

Given that my co-author spent the previous chapter ranting against *Scattergories,* I am reluctant to subject the reader to more harsh judgment. But I find it hard to disguise how much I dislike this game. *Scrabble* is like a math contest in which you can be rewarded for reciting pi to the thousandth decimal place without knowing that it expresses the ratio of a circle's circumference to its diameter. The word *egregious* is just a bunch of letters. It becomes beautiful and interesting only once you learn that it originates in the Latin words *ex grege*—out of the herd. For *Scrabble* people, however, it is simply an opportunity for eleven (or more) points.

I once tried to help my friend John Chew teach *Scrabble* to elementary school students in our neighborhood. My child (and his) were in the class, and I had hoped that the experience could kindle in my daughter a shared love for a game (even one that I did not like) that we could play together at home. I was immediately triggered by one of John's first handouts to the class, listing several dozen words that contain Q but not U, such as *qi.* I could scarcely conceive of a better symbolic reason for why I dislike *Scrabble.* The words in this category include qadi, qaid, qats, qoph, qajaq, and qabalah—words that no ordinary person would use at any point in life except to score *Scrabble* points. "You might as well tell us to memorize our neighbors' ATM-card PIN codes," I said to John after the session. "How is this *fun?*"

After many conversations with John and other *Scrabble* fans, I now know the answer to that last question. Which is not to say that I have learned to appreciate *Scrabble,* only that I now understand, in theory, why it brings joy to others. At least, I think I do. Joy, like every other human feeling, is something experienced internally, even if, in the case of *Scrabble*, the mechanism of stimulation takes place in a social milieu. As in the domains of music, sex, art, and food, one human mind can never truly comprehend the pleasure of another.

* * *

As a longtime *Scrabble* expert and top player who now makes his living supervising international tournaments and acting as a *Scrabble*-related media consultant, John was better placed than most to educate me about *Scrabble*. Moreover, he and I regularly play dozens of other games together. (Readers may recognize his name from my chapter on *Chinatown*.) Which is to say that gaming-wise, it is not as if he and I are creatures from different planets.

The majority of *Scrabble* fans, John explained to me, are people who enjoy the game on a casual basis. They do not spend their free time memorizing word lists. They have an innocent, playful approach to language, and love the simple act of forming letters into words in a competitive or social sphere. As a small child, this kind of player might have been the kid who looked at a STOP sign and told his parents that the same letters also can make POST, POTS, SPOT, TOPS and (if the child is precocious) OPTS.

To highlight the playful attitude to language that many *Scrabble* players indulge, John told me about a recent consulting project. "One challenge I had was to script the games played by the characters in Margaret Atwood's *The Handmaid's Tale* so that their plays would seem in character, yet still hit the necessary plot points in the television scripts," he tells me. "I did so by parsing all the words in the original novel, feeding them into a *Scrabble* analysis tool, then generating games using only Atwood's words, until I found ones that fit well." For most of us, this would be a crushingly boring exercise in data excavation. I am guessing that for John it was another day at the fun fair.

John has a background in postgraduate mathematics, which is not surprising. Many serious *Scrabble* players have a special interest in numbers. Their fixation on letter combinations often blurs the line between language, calculation, and puzzle-craft. One of John's U.S. counterparts, a tournament director named Dan Stock, delights in composing *Scrabble* pangrams (sentences using all one hundred *Scrabble* tiles exactly once each). These are often featured as large displays at the North American *Scrabble* Championship. A popular 1970s-era competition among *Scrabble* enthusiasts asked participants to find the smallest number of words required for such a pangram. (The winner completed the exercise with seven.) *Scrabble* players enjoy using letters in the same way that a child uses Lego.

Another analogy I have come to embrace for *Scrabble* lovers is that of the chemist in her lab, re-arranging atoms (letters) to produce molecules (words) that in turn are combined into useful products (sentences). And much like a *Scrabble* player who studies words without always dwelling on how they are used or what they mean, a chemist may not care what you put in your cocktail, so long as each alcohol molecule contains two carbon atoms, six of hydrogen, and one of oxygen.

I was shocked to learn that many of the world's top English-language *Scrabble* players do not speak English. In 2015, the New Zealand *Scrabble* legend Nigel Richards got so bored by demolishing opponents in English that he memorized a French dictionary and won the French-language *Scrabble* championships, although he still cannot order a sandwich in Paris. He and other top players exhibit a superhuman talent for memorization and spatial relationships (it does them little good to spell out long words if they are not able to do so in a score-maximizing way using "premium" tiles that double and triple the scores for individual letters or whole words).

I began to appreciate these finer points in 2016 when I accompanied John to the Canadian National *Scrabble* Championships.

Ottawa-area grandmaster Adam Logan defeated Vancouver's James Leong in the final match. Because spectators are not permitted in the finals gaming area, we all watched the action unfold on a video monitor in an adjoining room, where John provided expert real-time commentary.

The nature of his insights (as well as those of excited spectators who gasped and exclaimed at key moments) taught me a lot about how a big *Scrabble* brain works. As in chess, players must not only plan their own strategy but be mindful of their opponents' plans. An expert *Scrabble* player is constantly comparing the stock of played tiles to the full available inventory so as to assess the probability that he (or his opponent) will be able to draw this or that needed tile. And the best move is not always the one that maximizes this turn's score. It may be the one that sets the stage for a much larger bonanza further down the road.

The intellectual burden on *Scrabble* players may help explain why the game often can seem so tense, and why some players are driven to cheat. In 2017, Allan Simmons, a former British champion, was banned from competition after he was caught peeking at tiles before drawing them from the bag. An insider once told me an unsettling story of a contestant who tried to score an illegal word by taking advantage of his disabled opponent's difficulty in accessing the computer used to determine which words are admissible.

In *The Big Snit*, an iconic 1985 Canadian cartoon short about an elderly couple who fight bitterly (until finding love beyond the grave amid the ashes of nuclear war), the activity that almost destroys their love for all eternity is, you guessed it, *Scrabble*. One of the reasons the bickering at the heart of the plot seems so realistic is that *Scrabble* is, quite literally, a game built on pedantry: its mechanics are such that if your opponent plays a word you think is impermissible, you may "challenge" it. The stakes are high. As the rules specify, "If the play challenged is unacceptable, the challenged player takes back his or her tiles and loses that turn. If the play challenged is acceptable, the challenger loses his or her next turn." In our ordinary social and professional lives, we are taught that correcting people on their language is rude and anti-social. In *Scrabble*, pedantry is the key to victory.

"Way back in the previous century, I loved to play *Scrabble*," says Lawrence Dietz, a former editor for *Playboy* and *New West*. "We used Merriam-Webster's classic Second Unabridged edition, and it was a joy to challenge obscure words. [In that way], I often learned they existed—and their meaning.

"Then I met a woman who said she loved to play. We sat down at my house. She challenged a two-letter word I knew existed, and I carried over the Unabridged. [But] she icily brought the 'official' [*Scrabble*] dictionary out of her large tote bag. Naturally, the 'official' dictionary didn't have that word. She won that game, and a couple more. That took the pleasure from the game."

Different pedants will cite different sources. Writing in the *New Yorker*, Charles Bethea has pointed out that "Hasbro owns the game in North America, while Mattel owns it everywhere else. Hasbro has long had a publishing contract with Merriam-Webster, not Collins, and the company has little financial incentive to abandon that arrangement." As a result, players from different parts of the world are destined to disagree on which words are playable. A European or Australian player who plays by reference to *Collins Scrabble Words* (CSW) would have 276,663 acceptable words at her disposal. This presents an enormous disparity with the aforementioned Merriam-Webster *Official Scrabble Players Dictionary* (OSPD), which contains less than half that number. (Then there is the Tournament Word List which, at 192,111 entries, is its own creature. And a true pendant would take pains to note that the Collins list is actually a combination of the OSPD and the *Official Scrabble Words* list (OSW), which itself originated from the *Chambers Dictionary*. That original merger is known to *Scrabble* enthusiasts and experts as SOWPODS, a term that, in a masterpiece of irony, is deemed unacceptable according to *all* word lists.)

* * *

There are all kinds of games out there and what turns my crank does not have to turn yours. Amid this cornucopia, however, certain general principles apply. One of them is that a fun beer-and-pretzel game should have some mix of skill and luck. Backgammon is a classic example, as are many of the most popular card games. A game that is all luck and no skill, like *Snakes and Ladders* or *Unicorn Glitterluck*, is suitable only for small children. A game that is all skill and no luck, like checkers, Go, or chess, is always going to be less popular among couples and friends than at dedicated clubs where players can sort themselves by skill.

Those who like word games should try the 2015 breakout hit *Codenames*, in which "spymasters" take turns giving one-word clues to help their teammates target words arrayed on a game board; or *Paperback*, in which players take the role of novelists trying to make a deadline. Both feature a good mix of luck and skill. *Scrabble*, by contrast, involves just enough luck to disqualify it from the most exalted realms of mind-sport (which perhaps is why everyone knows the name Garry Kasparov but few know Nigel Richards), while the vast memorization requirements mean that veterans will always humiliate beginners, one of several reasons I stand by my original judgment of this overrated game.

But how much is my judgment worth? As my co-author argued in the latter paragraphs of her chapter on *Monopoly*'s Stupid Free Parking Rule, the only thing that matters about joy is whether or not it is felt. Everything else is blather.

In one of his minor masterpieces, *Lear, Tolstoy and the Fool*, George Orwell dissected Leo Tolstoy's strangely intense disdain for Shakespeare. After defending the Bard of Avon for a few pages, Orwell gets to the rub: "The most striking thing is how little difference it all makes. . . . There is no argument by which one can defend a poem. It defends itself by surviving, or it is indefensible. And if this test is valid, I think the verdict in Shakespeare's case must be 'not guilty.'" In this sense, I have learned, games are very much like poems. I have taken the time to share my insights on *Scrabble* with John on many occasions, and in great detail. Like other qabalistic Scrabble zomboids, John does not give a qapik for my frowny beatdowns. And I suspect that any other *Scrabble* fan reading this piece will share that attitude.

* * *

Every year, I attend a three-day Toronto convention called Breakout, which bills itself as "the best place for tabletop gamers of all kinds to get their game on and hang out with their community." Breakout is a great experience although it is a bit of a stretch to call the attendees members of a "community." Hobby-wise, board gaming is more properly described as a confederation of sub-communities, each defined by their particular gaming interests (a point that I will develop in this book's final chapter).

Since 2017, Breakout has been hosted at a large downtown hotel where different conference rooms are devoted to different types of games. The schedule of events contains hundreds of tournaments, sessions and meet-ups devoted to every imaginable game. In the main board-gaming hall, every table is its own little subcultural universe with, say, a group of heavy gamers playing an intense historical title such as *Indonesia* or *Pax Renaissance* seated just a few feet away from a group of casual drop-ins playing *Sushi Go Party!* or *Humpty Dumpty*. You could not pay me to join their games and I suspect, if the question were put to the others, they would feel much the same about mine. The equivalent in the music community would be a mash-up of micro-concerts, with groups of metalheads seated cheek-by-jowl with jazz fans and EDM aficionados.

One of the reasons I enjoy Breakout is the diversity on display. The organizers' self-declared goal is to "build a community space that includes all gamers. . . . We believe that a diverse range of experiences and perspectives is absolutely necessary for building a thriving and healthy gaming community." But when it comes to experiencing shared joy with other people, a critical rite of bonding and intimacy, the barriers that exist between people usually are not defined by categories such as race and sex. Sometimes, it comes down to habits of mind that cannot be changed or even fully understood by an act of will. To me, the act of memorizing words, and of spelling them out during a competitive contest, will always feel like a grim chore. Ultimately, that says more about me—and all of us—than it says about *Scrabble*.

CHAPTER THIRTEEN

Horrible People

*(Joan Moriarity: Lessons from
Cards Against Humanity)*

I N 1999, A SMALL WISCONSIN-BASED company called Out
of the Box Publishing released a game designed by Matthew Kirby
called *Apples to Apples*. It was a big box of cards, most of them
red, some green. The rules were simple. Each player would draw
a hand of seven red apple cards. Each of these cards had a word or
phrase printed on it. The word or phrase could be anything: "The
Great Pyramid of Giza," or "Socks" or "The JFK Assassination."
One player would be selected as a judge and the judge would draw
and reveal one green apple card. The green apple cards would each
have an adjective printed on them, like "Scary." Then everyone
except the judge would choose a red apple card from their hand and
put it face down on the table, trying to pick the one they imagined
the judge would think was most fitting for the green apple card—
in this case, the scariest. The cards would be mixed up so nobody
could tell which one had come from which player (thereby remov-
ing any *Scattegories*-style politics from play), and the judge would
read them aloud one at a time. Often, none of the players would
have a really suitable word so they would be forced to make odd

or creative choices. This kept the emotional stakes low. Part of the enjoyment lay in feeble attempts to justify the various combinations given – "actually, bunnies can be absolutely terrifying. Have you seen *Watership Down?*"

Once all the red apple cards had been revealed, the judge would announce the best choice, and whoever happened to be the player who contributed that card would score a point. Then the next player would become the judge, and process would repeat until someone scored a certain number of points.

Apples to Apples was a smash hit in its time. Anyone who could read the title could play the game. There were no right or wrong answers, so there was no chance of being made to feel stupid in front of family and friends. If you lost one round, it was easy to blow it off, attributing it to the judge's obvious lack of perspective ("If you had been six years old when you watched *Watership Down* you would understand.") Children, parents and grandparents could play together, and everyone had a chance to win. It sold in the millions, becoming so popular that in 2007 that Out of the Box was able to sell the rights to the game to Mattel just as the retail market for tabletop games was surging and games were beginning their long push back into the mainstream.

Unfortunately for Mattel, *Apples to Apples* would soon be totally eclipsed by another game. In 2009, *Cards Against Humanity* dropped on the tabletop market like a dirty bomb. Functionally it was almost identical to *Apples to Apples*. The only structural difference between the two games was that players would hold ten cards instead of seven. The cards were black and white instead of green and red, and the things printed on the cards were "edgy." Meaning they referred to bodily functions, various forms of debauchery, atrocities, and hot-button sociopolitical issues. So instead of bunnies or socks you got "An erection lasting longer than four hours" or "Dead babies."

In what may well be the most brilliant marketing move in the history of tabletop games, *CAH* billed itself on the box cover as "A party game for horrible people." I believe it was this phrase, more than anything else, that enticed millions of people to play it, even if they never thought they would be interested in games. *Especially* if they were uninterested in games. After all, nearly all of us think ourselves horrible sometimes. By granting its players permission to be horrible right there on the box, *Cards Against Humanity* was announcing that it was a game for everyone.

These sorts of who-wrote-what games have always been popular. At family gatherings, my father's relatives used to play one called *Fictionary*. One player would take a dictionary, open it to a random page, find a word none of the players knew (this might take a couple of tries) and then write down the definition. The other players would each invent a phony definition for the word, write those down, and pass them to the player with the dictionary. Then, one at a time and in a random order, all the definitions, real and fake, would be read aloud. On the second reading, the players would try to guess which was the real definition. They would score one point for guessing correctly, and one point for each other player who was tricked into guessing that their phony definition was the real one.

If this sounds familiar to you, there is a good chance you have played an almost identical game that was marketed and sold under the name *Balderdash* (1984), which is a fine example of what happens when enterprising individuals (in this case, designers Laura Robinson and Paul Toyne) think of a way to persuade customers to pay money for a game they could easily play for free. *Balderdash* is far from the only commercial title out there built on the foundation of that same public-domain parlor game my dad played with his family. Dozens of variations on the basic who-wrote-what structure populate the party-game sections of gift stores. Most of these games, however, have a problem with accessibility. They put players on the spot, requiring them to be clever on command. For my relatives, this was the main point of the exercise. For many others, the pressure of having to perform and improvise is not fun.

People who are terrible at drawing might experience a similar dread of playing *Pictionary*, and there have been a few drawing games that have sought to solve that problem, *Telstrations* chief among them. *Apples to Apples* provided a novel and effective solution to the problem with *Fictionary* and other similar "who wrote what" games. You do not have to invent anything. All you have to do is choose one of the seven cards from your hand and put it face down on the table, even if it makes no sense. Especially if it makes no sense! *Apples to Apples* lets players off the hook in a "who wrote what" challenge.

Cards Against Humanity goes one big step further. It also lets players off the hook for being horrible. It gives players permission to say shocking things with none of the consequences that would ordinarily ensue. It puts making a fart joke on the same moral plane as making a rape joke.

A friend of mine had a teenage stepdaughter. The two of them shared a warm friendship filled with laughter and a lot of good-natured teasing. He was playing *CAH* with friends and she asked to join in. Foolishly, he agreed. Her turn came. She drew a black card: "Why am I sticky?" Her preferred choice for the winning white card that round? "Date rape." Everyone laughed their heads off. It was so unfathomably inappropriate, they could not stop laughing no matter how much they wanted to.

The joyous release of being awful and saying awful things has an undeniable appeal, and it feels churlish to deny your fellow players that enjoyment. After all, if the whole box is full of content guaranteed to be sexist, racist, anti-Semitic, homophobic, transphobic, ableist, ageist, classist and otherwise objectionable, then all bets are off, right? Your white friend who feels deeply resentful that he cannot say the n-word without somebody telling him off? He can do it by proxy in this game (or at least he *could* have done it in earlier editions—more on this later) because somebody else wrote the card. He was just playing, right? And it says right on the box that the game is for horrible people. If you object to racism being played for laughs, you must be some kind of PC killjoy, right? And if you are the one person of color at a table full of white people, or the one woman at a table full of guys, or the one queer at a table of straights? The implication is that you had better not mention anything about any unpleasant feelings you are experiencing or you will ruin everyone's fun.

At another game night, one of the players was a survivor of child-hood sexual abuse. She had to hold back tears while her friends laughed uproariously at the mention of an act that, in real life, had wounded her in ways difficult to talk about. She could not quite manage to keep it inside and had to leave the table. Small wonder that some players at that game have no wish to play *Cards Against Humanity* again. Some of them.

The game has often been criticized for this "punching down" style of humor, using minorities, women, and children as punch lines. Within the board-game subculture, its creators, a group of eight friends who graduated from the same Chicago-area high school, were seen by some as callous, insensitive edgelords. Yet to the surprise of many, they did listen to at least some of the criticism they received, and acted on it. From one edition to the next, the creators have adjusted the cards to remove racial epithets, as well as jokes at the expense of rape survivors and others whose status makes them frequent targets of hate speech and violence. It certainly appears they would prefer to be seen as punching *up*, making fun of the powerful rather than the downtrodden. They even created a science-themed expansion set, the proceeds from which went to a scholarship pro-gram for women in STEM fields, and they produced a queer-themed expansion with proceeds going toward LGBTQ+ health resources.

The basic version of *CAH* is still capable of producing hurtful results, even after being toned down. The game could not be what it is without that possibility. You might ask how much harm has come from the game and whether or not charitable donations can atone for prior harm, considering how the money to afford those donations was amassed in the first place. These are fair questions, but I am not qualified to answer them.

Another curious thing about *Cards Against Humanity* is the people who choose to play it. I have spent years observing people selecting and playing games so I think I have a better sense than most about which games reach which target audiences. For a long time, I assumed it must be straight, white, cisgender dudes driving the game's massive success. As the years went by, I began to notice something about the people at the café who came to me looking for help finding a copy of it: roughly nine in ten were women, and about half of those were women of color. Obviously, I do not know and cannot know the exact reasons why people choose to play any particular game but I thought my experience had provided me with ample basis for making educated guesses. What I saw went against who I supposed this game was for and how it was meant to be enjoyed. I wondered who these women could be punching down at. Their queer friends? Their trans friends? That did not seem likely.

The creators of *CAH* got into some hot water for a Jewish-themed expansion pack. I doubt anyone was surprised to learn that jokes about the Holocaust went over poorly in some quarters. But the creators were also unsurprised by the popularity of the "Jew Pack" (yes, that's what they titled it) among their Jewish fans because they are Jewish themselves. My co-author has told me that I need look no further than this for my explanation, citing his friends' fondness for humming "Springtime For Hitler" as a means of robbing Nazi imagery of its power to hurt them, and using anti-Semitic imagery for fun and self-empowerment.

I believe that in the case of *CAH* the issue may be more complex. For example, Jon also mentioned that for many older Jews, the memory of the Holocaust is still too close for that kind of humor to work. And although I cannot speak for any ethnic group other than my own, my guess is that within most, if not all such groups there is a wide variety of opinion on the acceptability of such things. Even so, I wonder how it would feel to be the lone Jewish kid at the table when the black card came up: "War! What is it good for?" and your classmate chose "The Jews" as the winning white card. How about if your school was in Charlottesville? How about if the rest of the players were all Jewish too?

There are no easy answers to questions about whether or not this game is okay. The closest thing to an easy answer I have is "it depends who you play it with." If you are with people who have lived much the same kinds of experiences you have, you might not feel particularly worried about being singled out. And if there are lines you do not want crossed, there is a good chance your friends will know about them and will be careful not to cross them.

* * *

All that said, my biggest problems with *CAH* have nothing to do with how I would feel about punchlines directed at me or fears that my friends will not respect my boundaries. I take issue with the game itself and what it represents from a design standpoint. I hate *Cards Against Humanity* and would never willingly play it. This is not because of the hurt it can cause or how ubiquitous it has become (although it does get extremely dull hearing the same "shocking" phrases over and over again at work) but because it is simply not a good game. It is lazy and boring. *Apple to Apples* is not a great game either but at least there is some small degree of thought you need to put into your choice of which red apple card to play. For instance, if you think the judge is a logical sort, try appealing to their sense of reason ("Rabbits are terrifying to Australian farmers").

In *CAH*, it has been my experience that all you have to do is pick the most "shocking" white card in your hand. The text on the black card which you are supposed to be playing off is usually immaterial. Unless one of the other players had something in their hand that is more "outrageous," your answer will almost always be the "winner." That is how unimportant you are as a player in that game. It is a matter of taste, of course, but just as my co-author does not enjoy games that require excessive memorization, I do not like games that make me feel as though I might as well not even be playing.

A secondary reason I avoid *CAH* is my distaste for the effect it has had on the broader party game sector of the industry. Now that the template for a "shocking" version of a popular party game has been established, everyone wants in on the act and this annoys the hell out of me. You can now buy *Telestrations: After Dark,* which is *Telestrations* with "dirty" prompts for the initial drawings (and frankly, if you do not end up with a lot of dirty guesses over the course of a *normal* game of *Telestrations*, I question your commitment). There is an X-rated version of *Trivial Pursuit,* with adult-themed trivia questions and a little rubber stamp that you can use to mark a losing player's forehead with an X. *Anomia, Taboo, 5-Second Rule, Things in a Box, Codenames,* one after another every popular party game on the market is rushing to make an "adult" version of their perfectly enjoyable games, so they can throw it into a black box with white sans-serif text and watch it fly off the shelves. Someday, Mattel will no doubt publish an "adult" version of *Apples to Apples* and I will slap my forehead every time I hear somebody call it a rip-off of *Cards Against Humanity.*

Worse still, there is a flood of full-on *CAH* clones, all copying the original *Apples to Apples* formula of "everyone plays a card then one player picks their favorite." Each one is less original than the last, and their ongoing popularity drives me nuts. There's *What do you Meme* (*CAH* with internet memes), *Red Flags* (*CAH* with bad dating material), *Joking Hazard* (*CAH* with three-panel web comics), *Marry Blank Kill* (*CAH* with a lot of pointless complexity), and on and on. People devour these products despite the thousands of other, more interesting options out there (I know—broken record). Players must be getting some kind of enjoyment out of these games, even the ones trying to play them with only two players (I wish I were kidding but I see this every shift), or they would not keep coming back for the same experience over and over.

* * *

More than once in this book, I have danced around an issue that vexes many enthusiasts like me: if our beloved immersive, challenging games (like *Dead of Winter* for example) are so great, why are so many people so viscerally repulsed by the idea of even trying them? I am not exaggerating the revulsion. It is real and I see it all the time. Faces and body language speak louder than words. Actions speak louder still, and when I see people rejecting the kinds of games I love best in favor of a game famous for jokes about ethnic cleansing and date rape, I cannot help wanting to understand why.

On rare occasions, when my interaction with a group of players at the café feels especially warm and well-established, I ask them somewhat directly. The most common reason they give is "we don't want to have to think," or "we just don't want anything that's like strategy." People say this even when they have asked for a copy of *Connect Four*, a game that consists entirely of strategy and nothing else—where the player who thinks harder almost always wins—so I find those answers suspect. I believe it is not that they do not want to think but that they do not want to be seen to fail. That is only my guess, of course, but I believe this is true of most people who enjoy *CAH* while eschewing more demanding games: they do not believe that the magic circle, that barrier between the play space and the real world, will protect them when they make a mistake, and all too often they are right.

It is easy for me to tell people that it will be okay if they make dumb moves, that it will be fun to learn by trial and error. After all, none of the dumb moves I have ever made in a game have been taken as representative of the capabilities of my entire ethnic group. Someone with a different life experience might have something else to say about that.

People are taught different things about the consequences of failure. You might have seen that TED Talk on YouTube where Reshma Saujani speaks of an experiment conducted in the 1980s in which young boys and girls were tested with mathematical problems well above their grade level. The kids in this experiment were gifted students, the best in their classes. The boys found these problems challenging and invigorating, so they dug in. They did not necessarily succeed, but they tried. The girls, on the other hand, were more likely to give up, and the higher their grades were, the more likely they were to give up. Saujani also speaks of a study of job applicants. Men will apply for a job if they meet about 60 percent of the qualifications; women will not apply unless they meet almost 100 percent.

If you take a moment to think about it, the reasons behind their reluctance become clear. When boys try something and screw it up, they are often praised for their bravery and encouraged to try again. Girls? They are often criticized and made to feel like they are intruding where they do not belong. Under conditions like that, who wants to stick their neck out into a world of little wooden cubes and victory points representing the intellectual equivalent of a bloodsport? If you have been trained to expect to be given a hard time for trying something you are not guaranteed to succeed at, it only makes sense to shy away from such challenges.

Then there is the issue of race. All kinds of people play and enjoy games but the culture of the board game as hobby has been coded almost subconsciously as a thing for white guys. For a long time, the people depicted on game boxes and components were almost always white. The settings for games were typically in Europe or America or fantastical or science-fictional variations thereof, and when we did see depictions of people from other parts of the world, it was usually pretty easy to tell that they had not been created by people who were from those places (remember *Rising Sun* and *Legend of the Five Rings*?). For racialized people, games have often been full of this kind of subtle but powerful signal that this was not made for them.

The problems do not end with intimidation and representation. If you are a girl, or a person of color, and you discover that you love board games, fantasy, science-fiction, and so on, you can already expect sexism and racism from within the hobby; there is plenty of documentation of that depressing truth (run a quick Google search on "sexism," "racism," and "games" for an unpleasant glimpse). But the problems do not stop at the comic book store or the game club either. When you go home to your family, when you talk with your friends about your hobby, they might raise an eyebrow over why you would want to enter this world. To be clear, it is not my place to speak for people in that position. I would, however, recommend a piece written by Daniel Jose Ruiz in 2017 for *The Millions* called *"Dragons Are for White Kids with Money: On the Friction of Geekdom and Race."* It was a real eye-opener for me.

For years, I have struggled to find ways of convincing people to try the games that provide those wonderful, breathless moments of uncertainty where you cannot know if your efforts will succeed or fail until you see them play out—thrills and chills and unforgettable experiences with your friends. But no amount of describing those moments, no amount of persuasion or pleading will work on someone who does not believe that the magic circle will protect them.

Although I still encounter a lot of reluctance toward trying games for enthusiasts, that reluctance has been slowly waning year after year as players of all kinds begin to feel the inherent limitations of games like *Cards Against Humanity*. Even its most ardent fans agree that it gets dull after everyone has seen the cards a few times. Representation of diverse people in hobby games has also improved greatly over the past decade. A yearly game convention in Toronto called Breakout Con has been diligently building its reputation as a welcoming place for everyone who wants to play, through its promotional materials, harassment policy, and community outreach. As a result, Breakout sees thousands of diverse players enjoying all manner of games together every year. Tabletop game podcasts and YouTube series, which were the near-exclusive province of white guys just a few years ago are seeing many new and diverse voices.

There is still a long way to go. On the industry end of things, designers, developers, and publishers are still overwhelmingly white and male. Why is that? Any number of reasons. Gatekeeping, historical inertia, institutional prejudice—the answers could fill a book and I would need to do a lot more research to write it. I expect that over the coming decades, as the hobby gradually extends to a wider audience, the industry side will also be joined by a wider range of people with a passion for games.

In the meantime, low- or no-stakes games like *CAH*, where players can never experience failure or meaningful success, do serve a purpose. Despite their drawbacks, the magic circle can be very easy to draw and maintain among friends in such a game. Fear, judgment, and shame are kept at bay while you enjoy the play and one another's company. Some (like me) may take issue with *CAH*'s content but I am beginning to understand that many people who enjoy *CAH* fully understand and even agree with my arguments against it, and yet they choose to engage with that content anyway, on their own terms. They choose to draw their circle in a way that keeps out judgment and snobbery and just lets them play.

At least, that is how it appears to me today. I am just as eager to hear more voices in this conversation as I am to play new games and make new friends. Whether you love or hate *Cards Against Humanity*, I invite you to talk with your fellow players about these things, and if you feel so inclined, with me as well. Like the industry, I too have come a long way, and have a long way yet to go.

(Full disclosure: for quite some time, my employer was the primary Canadian distributor for Cards Against Humanity, *and as a result of this relationship, I have had a steady job.)*

CHAPTER FOURTEEN

Discovering Myself By Invading Belgium

(Jonathan Kay: Lessons from Advanced Squad Leader)

O N MAY 17, 1940, as Nazi forces pushed west toward the English Channel, a small group of Belgian infantry in the town of Kapelle-op-den-Bos tried to halt the Wehrmacht advance across the Willebroek-to-Brussels shipping canal. A crackle of Belgian machine-gun fire announced the onset of hostilities. Panicked German attackers bolted back to the eastern side of the main bridge, terrified by their first real taste of combat. The battlefield went still, for the moment.

Minutes later, German officers rallied their troops. Squads of combat engineers led the way forward with smoke grenades, and German anti-tank and machine gun positions provided covering fire. The bulk of the force inched forward, slowly expanding a small beachhead on the western side of the canal. It was all happening too slow for the attackers' purposes, however. Belgian reinforcements were known to be approaching, including a squadron of AMC35 tanks. The Germans' orders were to seize all of Kapelle-op-den-Bos that day. Even a small tactical setback in a single town could delay the wider offensive.

The German force now organized itself within a row of shops lining the western side of the canal, and began laying down fire against Belgian strongpoints. Meanwhile, the engineers who had spearheaded the initial assault made their way down side streets and alleys, seeking opportunities to ambush the reinforcements. Some encircled defenders lost heart, and began routing away. When a pair of Belgian tanks arrived from the west, street-fighting German infantry tossed grenades down the hatch of one and immobilized the second with an anti-tank rifle. Emboldened German rank-and-file began pushing forward from their positions, advancing into bloody house-to-house combat. Amid the chaos of battle, some Belgians surrendered. Others fought on before succumbing to force of numbers. A German victory seemed at hand.

Yet it turned out that not all the Belgians had given up the fight. With evening coming on, a small group of holdouts, last seen fleeing into a canal-keeper's office, had thrown up the Belgian colors atop a makeshift flagpole, and was now sniping at the Germans from the rear. It was just a few dozen men—a fraction of the attackers' strength—but until these stalwarts were dislodged, Kapelle-op-den-Bos could not be considered conquered territory. Muttering fiercely as his men made preparations to bed down under fire, the German battalion commander began composing his explanations to regimental headquarters. Finishing this mission would take his tired men at least one more day.

What I described in the paragraphs above did not actually happen. Yes, real German troops did attack the town of Kapelle-op-den-Bos on May 17, 1940. Nevertheless, my description of the battle is wholly imaginary. The blow-by-blow account originates in a board game called *Advanced Squad Leader* (*ASL*), in which players use realistic maps and hundreds of little cardboard tokens to refight battles

from World War II. Each game is called a "scenario," whose origi-
nating premise is sourced carefully from the actual fighting forces
and battlefield conditions that held sway as history unfolded. My
above-described experience as faux-German commander in Kapelle-
op-den-Bos emerges from a scenario called Belgian Tigers, designed
by Peter Stuijf and Chris Mazzei on the basis of surviving historical accounts from Belgian tank crews who fought that day. (In real
life, the Germans won a clear victory. In the game version, I was
eventually bested by an experienced Swedish player named Andreas
Carlsson at a 2017 ASL tournament in Copenhagen.)

While I have played hundreds of different tabletop games over
the years, like many enthusiastic gamers I have only one true love.
For some, this is *Scrabble*. For others, it is Go. Or *Monopoly*. Or
Dungeons & Dragons. For me, it is *ASL*. Always has been, since the
day I started playing it as a teenager. There is something about it that
speaks to me. I played casually with friends in school. As an adult,
now in middle age, I spend much of my leisure time traveling to
ASL tournaments in different parts of the world—Denmark, Israel,
Cleveland, Montreal. Tabletop gaming is an important part of my
life, right up there with family and work.

That is not to say that I regard the *outcome* of these games to
be important. I never gamble real money on the outcome. Even in
tournament play, I know that what I am doing has no more real-
world significance than a child's game of *tic-tac-toe*. While I am a
competitive person, and play to win, I take pains to ensure that my
games always end with a smile and a handshake. I also know that
gaming satisfies a variety of decidedly important human appetites—
which is why I have joined with my co-author, Joan Moriarity, to
write this book.

Every gamer brings a different set of appetites to the table
which is why there are so many different games. The sort of person
who loves, say, an empathy-driven social emulator such as *Dixit* is

unlikely to go in for a hard-core war game like *ASL*. A beer-and-pretzel college-dorm strategy gamer who enjoys swindling and ego-jousting his roommates is always going to prefer *Chinatown* over a cooperative game such as *Eldritch Horror*. A serious-minded, highly analytical intellectual usually will prefer the tightly controlled 8 x 8 arena of chess to the comic crash-and-burn mayhem of *Galaxy Trucker*. Tabletop gaming is not really one hobby. As I noted in my *Scrabble* chapter, it is a thousand hobbies, each with its own rich and growing subculture.

So what is it about *ASL* that appeals to me? Those first few paragraphs should give you a clue. I am not just playing a game when I play: I am telling a story. In a perfect world, I would not have to go to airless conference rooms in Copenhagen or Cleveland to produce stories through the manipulation of little cardboard counters. I would be able to do it the way Tolstoy and Proust did it—scribbling away in a notebook. I have tried that, and it does not work for me. I am not a fiction writer. I try to create characters and breathe life into them. They stare back at me from the page, shrugging, shuffling around listlessly. They have no inner momentum or urgency to their actions, and so I find myself paralyzed, not being able to pick from the infinity of possible actions and thoughts that I may ascribe to them.

When I play a board game—especially a richly detailed one such as *ASL*, the motivation is clear. It is written in the "victory conditions" for each scenario. I have to take a bridge, destroy a bunker, clear a town. That fictional battle in Kapelle-op-den-Bos emerged over seven hours and hundreds of dice rolls. All the little details from the fight would have been impossible for me to conjure out of thin air. Yet within the context of a rules-bound game, Andreas and I created a sort of action-movie screenplay by accident. We did it as a team, collaboratively and spontaneously, the way a jazz ensemble creates a new tune. Going in, neither of us had any idea how the movie would end, only how it would begin.

When people ask me why I never watch TV or movies, I tell them it is because board gaming takes up all my free time. That is not the whole truth. It is also the case that the experience of passively watching video bores me. After experiencing the thrill of midwifing a story right then and there on a tabletop, I refuse to go back to a form of entertainment that requires me to sit back and watch someone else's fully formed story pop out of a box.

Realistic war games such as *ASL* also bring history alive by putting players in the shoes of the generals and forcing them to act out the strategic choices faced by both sides. As a Jew whose ancestors were slaughtered by the Nazis, I know something about the crimes against humanity perpetrated by Hitler and his minions. I will admit that it has felt strange to take the German side in a war game but even that sense of unease has its educational side. Notwithstanding the monstrous nature of the Nazi regime, the young men who took up arms for the regime were flesh-and-blood human beings whose manner of warfare shaped the history of Europe. They, and their ways, deserve study for their own sake.

I also am cognizant of the great privilege I experience, living in a peaceful country such as Canada, where I can experience the simulation of war as an intellectual pursuit. When I play *ASL*, I am mindful of this. No matter who wins or loses a scenario, there always are plenty of dead on both sides. It shocks me to push myself back from the board and think that hundreds of men actually did die to capture or defend some meaningless piece of real estate. Playing *ASL* has, in this way, turned me into something of a pacifist.

It was not just the Nazis who regarded life as cheap. I have played 1945-era *ASL* scenarios in which I have "commanded" some of the Red troops who served Stalin's totalitarian USSR and brutalized the citizenry of Berlin. In another scenario, set in October 1937, two years before World War II even started, I commanded elements of the Japanese Expeditionary Army that descended upon the Chinese

88th Division holed up in Shanghai's Zhabei district, and massacred them down to a man.

While Nazism was a uniquely malignant force in world affairs, a close study of the period shows that evil came into full bloom in many countries, and under the banner of many movements. And so the only way to immerse oneself in any kind of military re-enactment is to compartmentalize the tactics from the underlying causes they served. Again, this is not for everyone. But that is why there is *Jenga*.

Are board gamers "nerds"? It is hard to generalize but I would say that, yes, during our high school years, a lot of us spent more time in a science club than as an athlete or Casanova. Speaking for myself, I had difficulty making friends as a child, in part because I spent a lot of time bedridden with asthma. Even now, as an adult, I have difficulty sustaining conversations that are not about topics that interest me intellectually. I grow bored if I am not taxing my brain in some way. (One of the defining aspects of *ASL* is that it is extraordinarily complex which, paradoxically, is its main source of appeal for many ardent players. As my gaming friend Andy put it to me once, after an especially intense game: "This is the only thing I do in life that occupies 100 percent of my brain—that shuts everything else out.") Board gaming in general, and *ASL* in particular, is the only thing I do in life that allows me to fuse fully my desire for intellectual stimulation with the inborn human appetite for some form of social connection.

It goes beyond that: *ASL*, like all table top games, provides players with a path to self-improvement, so long as you are alive to the lessons of the game board. Why, for instance, did I ultimately lose the fight for Kapelle-op-den-Bos? When I play the battle back in my head, I realize that I had become so elated by the prospect of victory I carelessly forgot to assign troops to mop up defenders in the rear. This has been a recurrent issue for me in *ASL*: I fall behind in a game, then summon up all my intellectual strength to turn the tide, only to lose at the end when I become cavalier. Moments such as this make me wonder if this is something I also do in "real life."

By keeping careful track of my game results over the years, I have noticed other trends. I do better in morning games than evening games, in part because I forget to eat food or drink water when I experience stress, and sometimes become fatigued or even dizzy late in the day. I prefer attacking over defending. I try to anticipate my opponents' moves by putting myself in their shoes—but often have difficulty doing so. (Why? A failure in my empathic capabilities, perhaps?) Like all players, I sometimes blame losses on bad luck, yet take full credit for my victories. The *ASL* game board is not just an arena of war. It is an arena of ego, of temperament, of human strengths and foibles. Learning important life lessons often can be painful or humiliating. With *ASL*, it is fun.

One of the defining elements of the human animal is its capacity for abstract visualization. Other creatures are better than us at smelling, biting, hunting, running. We alone can create whole universes in our heads based on nothing more than thought. This is the basis of language, math, science, everything that defines human civilization. It is something monkeys and dolphins will never have.

When evolutionary theorists seek to explain how this capacity for abstract thought arose, the story often goes like this Our ancestors, beset by all sorts of deadly horrors in the African savannah, needed some way to anticipate risks before the moment those risks jumped out of the bushes, red in tooth and claw. So began the slow process by which the neural networks in our head, under pressure from the ruthless mechanism of natural selection, created the means to model risk before the risk manifested itself. What would happen if I went to forage for berries in that field and a lion appeared? Would I be able to make it to the protection of that outcropping? How many berries would I be able to get? How hungry am I? Is it worth the risk? Out of these habits of mind grew the whole mental apparatus by which we play out life scenarios as a game within our mind, before putting life and limb on the line in a true sense. The relationship between board games and real life is in some ways close.

Which brings me back to Kapelle-op-den-Bos. When that game was over, and Andreas and I had shaken hands, I confessed to him my shame at squandering victory in such a silly way. Andreas did not condescend to me. He agreed that my failure to guard the rear positions had cost me the game. He also noted, truthfully, that in a long match such as this, it is inevitable that some errors would be made.

Indeed, Andreas had made some mistakes of his own. As we went through our post-game analysis, scrutinizing the criteria that each of us needed to achieve for victory, it became clear that Andreas had not studied the scenario with sufficient care. In particular, he did not realize that the destruction of his tanks had been one of my listed objectives. Suddenly, I realized why he had deployed his tanks in such an aggressive, even careless manner. Had the dice come up differently in the final moments of our game, he, not I, who would have rued his carelessness. When I pointed this out to Andreas, he slapped his forehead and swore in Swedish.

Then he did something important: he laughed. Long and hard. And in that moment, I realized why. This is a lesson that comes back, full circle, to what my co-author has concluded from showing thousands of people how to play games at Snakes & Lattes. In games, as in life, if you beat yourself up for any deviation from a self-imposed standard of perfection, you will be an unhappy person. The happiest people I know are not those who come closest to perfection in their personal lives or their professions. They are the ones who give an honest effort in everything they do but forgive themselves when they come up short. Failure becomes an opportunity for self-improvement, not self-recrimination.

Of course, laughter is not always a socially appropriate response to failure. Sometimes, mistakes we make cause inconvenience or even real pain to the people around us. Which is why it is so especially gratifying to enter the world of board gaming where, win or lose, laughter is never inappropriate, because no one on either side gets shot or goes bankrupt, and the lion never gets his human prey.

That is the world of the tabletop, a place where many of life's great lessons leave their mark—but the sting never lasts longer than the time it takes to put all those little pieces back in their box.

CHAPTER FIFTEEN

Power Fantasies and the Power of Fantasies

(Joan Moriarity: Lessons from Dungeons & Dragons)

M Y FIRST *Dungeons & Dragons* character was a cleric. I was about ten years old. I did not understand what a cleric was but it sounded more interesting than being a fighter, thief or magic-user (which was the game's term for wizards back then). What I really wanted was to be like the lady in the red dress on the cover of the game box, who held a torch in one hand and a ball of magical green fire in the other, ready to throw it at a giant serpent creature, but I was not ready to deal with that yet. Instead of specializing in fighting abilities, magic spells or sneaky skills, clerics were a kind of warrior-priest. They could fight a little and they also had healing magic and a strange power called "turn undead."

"Undead" was my new word for the day, and I was excited to discover that there was a single term I could use to refer to all the different kinds of monsters that were sort of alive and sort of dead, like skeletons, zombies, vampires and ghosts. I wondered what I could "turn" them into.

Role-playing games (or RPGs) such as *D&D* are, in essence, a highly structured form of pretend, with a set of rules and charts you can use to determine whether you succeed or fail at all the various things you might try to do in the game's imaginary world, like fighting a dragon or avoiding a deadly trap. Playing "cops and robbers" can be frustrating when players cannot agree on whether you hit or missed them in a pitched gun battle. The rules and systems of a role-playing game are there to resolve those disputes.

Typically, each member of a group of players will create a character that exists within the fictional world of *D&D*, and those characters will go off on heroic adventures together. Their human creators sit around a table, describing what their characters say and do, just like in any other game of pretend. All except one player, who takes on the job of being the all-powerful Dungeon Master (or "referee" as they were sometimes called, way back when the game was commonly played in tournaments). The Dungeon Master (DM) plays the role of everyone else in this imaginary world of magic and danger. The DM's main responsibility is to entertain the players by throwing interesting challenges at them, typically in the form of wrongs that need heroes to put them right. This is heroic fantasy after all. The world isn't going to save itself.

I did not have enough friends to play *D&D* in the way it was intended back then. Andrew, the older kid who lived across the street, had the books and the dice and stuff, and was willing to be my DM. He also owned a couple of pre-made adventures (typically called "modules") for me to try, complete with enemies and other challenges to defeat. The baddies in these modules were calibrated to pose a challenge to a group of several adventurers working together, not a solitary hero. I did not know this at the time so I went in with all the optimism you might expect of a kid on that first exciting journey.

After speaking with some troubled townsfolk, I traveled to a dangerous abandoned keep and the first enemies I encountered there were skeletons, walking about and brandishing weapons. I was severely outnumbered but I remembered my ability to turn undead. I rolled a few dice and fortune smiled upon me. Andrew told me that I had successfully turned most of them to my side, and my new allies joined me in the battle against their erstwhile companions. We were victorious.

I felt a little strange about seeing these creatures fight against their own kind. I asked them if they were okay. They assured me they were fine. Together we explored the keep, discovering its mysteries and fighting the evil creatures who had taken up residence there and had used the place as a base for assaults against passing caravans and nearby villages. Whenever a battle seemed imminent, I would turn to my skeletal friends and remind them that the fight would be dangerous, and that they did not have to do this if they did not want to. They seemed to appreciate my honesty and stayed by my side. All of them fought bravely, and some of them gave their unlives to defeat the evil they had once been a part of. My first *D&D* adventure was a triumph.

It was not until almost a year later that I discovered the cleric's turn undead ability does not make undead turn away from evil. It just makes them recoil in fear from the cleric's holy presence for a little while. Andrew had never played or DMed for a cleric before and had never read the details of that particular ability. I think he was embarrassed when I told him. I was never supposed to be an autonomous evil-conversion and heroic recruitment office. It had been fun though.

Sometimes, when my mother and I traveled to the east coast to visit her family, I had some one-on-one adventures with my cousin

Matthew. He was well versed in the game. He had lots of characters he had created over the years, and many of those had accumulated extraordinary hoards of powerful magical items and weapons. Armed and equipped with that kind of gear, his characters were strong enough to take on even the toughest villains the game had to offer. I could not imagine the kinds of awesome encounters he must have survived to gain such treasures.

I had not been there for all that though, and we wanted to start a new game together. We also wanted to take on serious challenges so we made up four new heroes, figuring that Matt could control all of them together as if he were four players, and I could be the DM.

In those days, the process of creating a hero character in *D&D* would involve rolling a bunch of dice to determine how strong, how fast, how smart your character was. That seemed unfair to us. What if we ended up with a weak or slow or stupid character? I knew that some other kids at my school played *D&D*, and I knew some of their characters had gotten killed by relatively weak monsters because of unlucky dice rolls. Matt and I reasoned that if we played long enough and saw enough of our characters killed, after starting over and over again with new characters, eventually we would get lucky and roll up a group of godlike heroes with perfect or near-perfect stats. Instead of putting ourselves through all that trouble and heartache, we kept rolling up new characters until we had our ideal group.

Before long we discovered that such a group would be statistically improbable and it could take days of rolling dice to get what we wanted. We modified the system to make it less improbable. Why wait for the sake of waiting? It was a statistical inevitability that we would eventually get there, so we sped up the process a little. Modern versions of *D&D* (and other role-playing games as well) typically use a more egalitarian system in which each player is given a set number of points to spend on their various attributes, with greater power in any given area costing more points. If you are extremely charitable, you could say Matt and I were ahead of our time.

In the deeply silly adventures that followed, we proceeded to tear through the various big baddies presented in the *Dungeons & Dragons Monster Manual*, and we felt so proud of ourselves. The weakest member of our group of characters (who unlike any of the others actually had one ability score with a lowly sixteen out of a possible eighteen) was usually assigned to test the various magic items we found. This often came at great risk to his own health, as these items were frequently potions that could not be identified without taking a sip. Among our four incredibly dull, overpowered heroes, he was the one who came closest to having an actual personality. He was the one the others appreciated most of all. I am not sure what kind of lesson I learned from that, or if I had the wit to learn from it at all, but the seed was planted that it is not always the most powerful characters who are the most memorable or the most beloved.

Still, we reveled in the ludicrous power of those characters to crush one enemy after another. I would later learn that there was a disparaging name for *D&D* campaigns that resulted in the heroes acquiring endless riches and unstoppably powerful magical treasures. They call it "Monty Haul." When I heard the name, I was both amused by the pun and aware that I had been enjoying precisely that kind of stupid game. I felt a little embarrassed but my love for the crazy power fantasy was not entirely snuffed by the knowledge that some people looked down on that sort of play. It was fine if that was the experience you wanted, I supposed.

At the time—this was the early 1980s—a lot of parents were becoming concerned about the effect *D&D* might be having on kids. There were sensationalist media pieces about how the game promotes Satanism and suicide and, I dunno, listening to heavy metal or something. My mom was too smart to believe any of that. I did go through a brief and ill-advised heavy metal phase (no genre of music could have been a worse fit for my temperament), but she was pleased by how I could use words like "chaotic" or "probability" in a sentence, and she knew I had learned those from the game.

* * *

I was always a sensitive kid who could never grasp the concept of good-natured teasing so I had trouble relating to a lot of other children. I could not understand how it was possible to insult someone unless you actually meant for them to suffer emotional harm. The kids in my class were mean to each other all the time, and most of them seemed fine with it. Unlike them, I took everything to heart. Naturally this made me the ideal target, placing me squarely at the bottom of the pecking order. I hated them and they hated me but those kids were all I had, and the ones who liked *D&D* had few options besides me. Lacking alternatives, they let me play in their games.

I could not understand why the boys (and they were all boys) were always sneering at me for wanting to play feminine characters. On some level, I must have understood that it was not okay to play as a girl. In most schoolyards, just about the cruelest thing you can say to a boy is that he's like a girl. Whenever a character of mine demonstrated some kind of emotion that went any deeper than "let's kill that monster and take its treasure," I received similar derision. On one particular adventure, I was provided with a pre-generated character, a dwarf who had been a kind of mentor figure to a younger half-elven character in the group (spot the reference, *Dragonlance* fans). When my half-elven protégé announced his intention to do something dangerous, I felt concerned and asked him if he was sure it was worth the risk. To me, it did not seem weird but judging by the looks on the others' faces I was the only one who thought so. In retrospect, I doubt any of them had actually read their character's background sheet beyond the numbers assigned to their abilities and weapons.

Mostly I played with one particular kid and he was way better at creating fantasy worlds than I was. He knew I liked female characters in stories, and I really wanted to impress a certain woman bounty hunter in the imaginary world of the game we were playing. In the process, my character ended up making an absolute fool of himself. It is embarrassing to this day to think about it.

We played a simple game of hide and seek, you see. I had a head start, and as long as she did not find me within a few hours, I would win. I traveled all through the weird fictional city the DM described, deliberately passing through one gross and disgusting place after another, reasoning that she would not be willing to follow the trail if it led through sewers fouler than anything that existed in the real world. After all that, I hid in a smuggling compartment aboard a ship. Soon after I began to wait, I could hear a set of footsteps approaching, along with a soft pinging sound. There was a knock on the hidden door of the compartment. She had been tracking an object I was carrying with some kind of device. I knew it was all fictional. I knew there was no actual badass lady bounty hunter I wanted to impress, and there were no sewers overflowing with offal and fecal matter but, at the time, it felt like I had humiliated myself in front of a girl I had a crush on.

I spent a lot of time in video arcades at that age, too. The games in those days all required 25-cent coins to play them. Change machines were not common. There was usually a bored person behind the counter changing dollars for quarters. It was the kind of job that would make anybody desperate for distraction so I should not have been surprised when the guy at the arcade in the spiffy red vest and bow tie offered to DM me through a short adventure when he found out I played *D&D*. We played it right then and there at the counter.

I was dumbfounded at the idea of playing without the reference books, character sheets or dice. Without even a proper table or chairs. In just a short time, he showed me that imagination was much more important to a good role-playing game than any physical accouterments. I also learned that skill with systems and understanding of the rules mattered far less than creativity and cleverness.

This was decades ago but I still remember it clearly. My character almost immediately got into a terrible scrape. Despite having been given an extraordinary array of advantages, including a coveted "Holy Avenger" sword whose powers were truly fearsome in the hands of my chosen character type, I quickly found myself out of my depth. As I made one mistake after another, my Dungeon Master kept finding clever ways to drop me into hopelessly silly situations rather than killing me outright. My poor choices had consequences but the story could continue from there. To me, that guy with the red vest seemed like the coolest, smartest, most creative person in the world. I never saw him again.

* * *

As much as I had enjoyed those Monty Haul sessions with my cousin, I hungered for something more intense and dramatic, like the cartoons I used to watch on TV. I wanted the heroes and villains to be more like actual characters in a story, not just playing pieces on a board. I wanted so badly to travel to other worlds that I would create physical props replicating the treasures from those places.

There exists in the world of *D&D* a peculiar magical item called The Deck of Many Things. It is like a deck of tarot cards, only weirder and creepier. When your character draws a card from the deck, some random magical thing happens. It can be amazing (you become massively wealthy) or horrible (you are trapped in an extra-dimensional jail) or something in between (you will know the answer to your next dilemma). The rule book has a little chart for using a regular pack of cards to simulate this (Ace of spades? Imprisoned!). I wanted a deck with the names of the Many Things in it, so I made one of my own with cardboard and magic markers, complete with a slipcase to hold them. While I was not the most talented tween artist, I was proud of the result and had a lot of fun doing it. My budding interest in design showed itself through that little project.

Eager to see the deck appear in games I played as Dungeon Master, my Deck of Many Things would find its way into the treasure vaults of whatever enemies were lurking in my imaginary worlds. It never occurred to me to wonder why those villains never thought to use the deck themselves. Perhaps they were smarter than the child version of me.

D&D was certainly not the only roleplaying game out there, even then. A few short years after its publication, many other games explored different themes and settings for new adventures. *Gamma World* was a game of post-apocalyptic survival. *Top Secret* brought James Bond-style spycraft to the table. There were many others, and the original *D&D* itself branched out into new genres, pushed by writers and designers eager for variety and experimentation.

I got hold of a *D&D* adventure module called *Ravenloft*. While most *D&D* adventures were sword-and-sorcery yarns in the vein of *Lord of the Rings*, this was a tale of Gothic horror. It was set in a gloomy realm of fog and doubt, inspired by Eastern European folk tales, and the villain was a vampire named Count Strahd von Zarovich. You could say he was a *D&D* Dracula knock-off, but that would do a disservice to the love and care brought to *Ravenloft* by its writers, Tracy and Laura Hickman. They wanted to bring fantasy adventure to a different level. They wanted an adventure that told a proper story about more than defeating monsters and taking their treasure and getting more powerful so as to be able to take on bigger

monsters and claim their treasure, too. The idea was electrifying to
me. As soon as I saw it, I knew I had to try it.

My efforts were doomed from the start, though. None of the other
kids in my class were interested in all that airy-fairy story stuff. They
wanted to kill things. For them, being a pure-of-heart Paladin was
a matter of slaughtering everything in sight as long as it was "evil."
Questions about what it really means to be good or evil were for losers.
All the same, none of those kids really enjoyed being the Dungeon
Master so when I invited them to play *Ravenloft*, several accepted. By
this point, I was about fourteen and the stakes were simultaneously
lower and higher than a few years before. For them, bullying me had
lost its novelty. Although I was still beneath them in the social hierar-
chy, it was not always torture for me to be around them. And like any
kid, I wanted to impress my peers. I wanted to be liked.

I felt certain that if I allowed them to bring characters of their
own design with them, I would be greeted with a party of adventurers not so different from the boring, invincible superheroes my
cousin and I had created years before. So I created a cast of seven
adventurers whom I believed to be well suited to the difficulty of
the challenge set before them. I also drew pictures of them, and I
thought some of them looked pretty cool. I created back stories too,
which had embedded within them the seeds of what would surely
become a power struggle within the group at a key point in the story,
when the heroes' need for unity would be at its height.

Also, two of the characters were women, which did not sit well
with my players, all boys. For them, it was the height of ignominy
to play a female character. The ones who bothered to read what I
had written about their characters found amusing (and admittedly
somewhat clever) ways to mock the material. In fairness to them,
my writing was mawkish. Had my adult self been witness to those
proceedings, she would have been hard-pressed to keep a straight
face when that prose was read aloud.

One of the characters, a paladin of the evildoer-killing sort mentioned above, owned a powerful magic sword. In the picture I had drawn of him, his sword had vaguely Nordic-looking runes inscribed on the blade. I discovered at the end of one of our play sessions that the boy playing that character had written over the runes with the name he had apparently given to the sword: "!EVIL FUCKER¡" Even as uptight and defensive as I was, I couldn't help laughing at that.

Game day arrived, and I had prepared myself as well as I knew how. Early in the story, there was a gothic-fantasy version of a Romani fortune-teller for the protagonists to meet. This creepy old lady would instruct them on the frightful nature of the world around them and foreshadow the scary encounters that lay in store. I had rehearsed her creepy old lady voice and was ready to unsettle the crap out of those rowdy kids and put the fear of Strahd into them. I got two words in before the groans drowned me out. They insisted I speak normally. Again, in fairness, my teenage self's idea of an old crone's voice was probably too screechy and annoying to bear. Still, every attempt I made to bring some kind of gravitas or narrative to the game was being stymied by these uncouth boys who only wanted to kill monsters and get loot.

When the time came for our second session, less than half the players from the first one showed up. I tried to engage them with atmosphere, character, and narrative. Once again, they did not care. And then they found the Deck of Many Things.

Seasoned Dungeon Masters know something I did not know at that time: you should never, ever allow your players to acquire a Deck of Many Things because it kills stories dead. Even when those stories involve a tormented vampire lord in a Gothic horror setting, lovingly created by earnest writers who wanted to elevate *D&D* to a level of sophistication and pathos it had not been generally thought at the time to possess. The Deck does not care, and the pointless, nonsensical plot twists it produces will bring any drama, no matter how well constructed, to a screeching halt. But this time, there was no story to kill. And the result was the most bizarre and inexplicable success I had experienced since that first time I turned undead.

They started pulling cards and their sighs of boredom transformed into gleeful cackling. Up until that point, nothing had been at stake for the players. None of them were invested in anything that seemed likely to happen in that imaginary world. They did not care about the villain, and indeed they never actually encountered him. They did not care about the people held in his sway. They did not care about the oppressive fog that had descended on the land. They did not care about the missing children and despairing families of the town that cowered eternally in Strahd's malevolent shadow. But they did care about the weird killer demon thing that suddenly appeared in the air above them when they pulled a card from the Deck.

They gained and lost fortunes, were crushed into the void and resurrected by magical wish-granting. The same obnoxious teenage boys who moments before had been too hung up to use a game piece shaped like a girl were hugging each other and cheering at their salvation and losses, all because of a home-made deck of pretend tarot cards. By accidentally transforming the game from a sincere attempt at storytelling into the silliest Monty Haul scenario imaginable, the day was saved and my players had fun.

It was the first time I had been able to entertain a group of players who were not my blood relatives as a Dungeon Master. It taught me the single most important rule any DM can learn: give the players what they want. Even if it is stupid.

Later on, I would learn trickier lessons, involving issues of what the players want versus what they *think* they want, or what they *say* they want. I would learn from my fellow players, from other Dungeon Masters, and, perhaps impossibly from the fictional characters I played. One of those taught me that it was possible for someone as unlikely as myself to live honestly as a transgender woman. But that story, and many others, will have to wait for another time.

An Epistolary Epilogue

(Lessons from this book)

JK: Joan, it's now January 2019—exactly a year since you and I sat down at Snakes & Lattes (fittingly) to hash out an outline for this book. Since then, we've both played a lot of games, and written a lot of chapters. Now that the first draft of the book is in front of us, let me ask you: is this the book you originally thought we'd produce?

JM: Well, the format is pretty much in line with the idea you brought to me a year ago, and the list of game titles isn't too far off from what I figured it would be. Some chapters turned out as I expected. But several of them went in surprising directions. I mean, if you had told me back then that I would be writing a halfhearted defense of the Stupid Free Parking Rule, I would never have believed you.

How about you?

JK: There were a few things that took me by surprise. But the biggest was the degree to which the project ended up feeling *personal*. In my head, this was going to be a book in which I stood apart from the games and analyzed them in a dispassionate way. But my own personality and feelings kept getting in the way.

Take my chapter on *Monopoly*—the one in which I write about that game as a microcosm of unstable dynamical systems. I thought *all* my chapters were going to consist of wonky, arm's length analysis like that (with the exception of the *Advanced Squad Leader* chapter, which I knew would have a personal dimension, but which I imagined would be a sort of one-off personal tell-all). Board games are hermetically sealed little worlds, and I imagined that each chapter I wrote would, likewise, tell a hermetically sealed little lesson.

But real life kept asserting itself. Two of my chapters, for instance, deal with cultural appropriation and my own relationship to other cultures—subjects that inevitably caused me to examine my own identity as a man, Jew, white person and journalistic observer. Or take my chapter on *Scrabble*—which originally was supposed to be just a long screed about why I hated the game. As I wrote it, I inevitably started looking inward. *Why* do I hate it? Why do any of us "hate" anything?

I wouldn't say that writing the book was an act of *therapy* per se. But I definitely learned a lot about myself that I didn't know. And I'm wondering if the same was true of your experience.

JM: There were some pretty significant revelations, yes. Most of them had to do with the uncomfortable realization how narrow my particular bubble is when it comes to games and play. You wouldn't think so, given what I do for a living, but it's true. It's easy to believe uncharitable things about people who play games I hate, as long as I don't ever have to spend time talking with them about the subject in any depth.

When it comes to things like sociopolitical opinions, all I need is one YouTube search and I've got thousands of opinions, most of them very different from my own. But it's hard to find people talking about why they don't feel comfortable playing games that might seem a little challenging. So for years and years my thoughts on this were based on intellectual assumptions and workplace observations, because that was all I had to go on. As a result, I had a ton of wrongheaded ideas, and I know I still do, though hopefully a few less than before.

The biggest thing I've come away with is an intense desire to look closer, dig deeper, learn more about other people's attitudes and approaches when it comes to play. I want to talk with professional poker players and athletes and find out if they would still find their games worth playing at a high level if they couldn't earn a living at it. I want to explore the connection between roleplaying games and expressive art therapy. I want to get to the heart of the stigma against playfulness and find ways to break it. I want to talk with people from different cultural backgrounds to learn about how that stigma presents itself in different places around the world, and within different communities in my own city. And it's terrifying, because I'm not a researcher and I have no idea how to begin that process.

JK: The experience of researching all these games made me feel terror, too—but of a different nature. My own terror feel arises from the fact that I will die (or go senile) before I play 1 percent of the games that I want to play. This book covers a few dozen titles in some detail. But in the course of writing it, I examined hundreds of others (some of which are mentioned in passing). Many of these look fascinating to me. But I only have, at most, thirty or forty more years of gaming life in me. So cruel arithmetic tells me that I will probably never get around to simulate, say, the 1859 Battle of Magenta between French and Austrian forces during the Second Italian War of Independence. In fact, my life may be over before I ever get to simulate *any* battles from the Second Italian War of Independence. Which sucks.

As with all things, it comes back to the tragically finite nature of human existence and my own fear of death. Perhaps one of the reasons I like to immerse myself in hyper-complex games is that it distracts me, if only for a few hours, from the void of eternal blackness that awaits me beyond the grave.

But lest we end on too cheery a note, let me get back to your "uncomfortable realization [as to] how narrow my particular bubble is when it comes to games and play." This gave me pause. You are a professional board game guru at a large gaming café. You literally meet, and teach, hundreds of different gamers every month—people of all interests and abilities. Are you suggesting that these arm's-length pedagogical interludes don't really count when it comes to truly exposing yourself to other games and gaming styles?

JM: The arm's-length thing is actually a huge improvement on the way things were before I started the game guru job. Nearly everyone who's heavily vested in a particular art form tends to look down on those who approach it more casually—even if they make a big show of doing otherwise—and I was no exception. I once considered just about all the popular games to be beneath me, and it shames me to admit that on bad nights, that would extend to thinking of the people who played them as beneath me.

As the years went by and I watched those people having undeniably great fun playing those games week in and week out, it did have a softening effect on that snobbery, but when those same people rejected my other suggestions for no reason I could understand, that could bring it all back. And how better to defend your feelings against such rejection than to armor yourself with arrogance and superiority?

It's not a helpful response, obviously. But I think it's a very common coping mechanism among our kind. And it's sabotaging our efforts to bring play back to the world. In the course of co-writing this book, I've made an effort to look beyond my insecurities and try to view play from the point of view of someone outside our little subculture. I would love to have had the chance to talk to more people directly about this, but it's like pulling teeth trying to get any-one to open up about it. And even when people *are* willing to talk, they usually stick to facile answers like "I just don't want to have to think," or "It's too much effort," even when they clearly derive great enjoyment from other things in their lives that require an enormous amount of thinking and effort, like traveling, cooking, athletics, family, friendships, creative pursuits, pretty much anything that's really worthwhile.

Even though I did write a chapter about how *Scattergories* is a Satanic plot to destroy family life, I feel like I've genuinely come to a better understanding of the reasons why people choose not to immerse themselves in play, or at least, in certain kinds of play. I feel like I've come just far enough to realize how much farther I have yet to go, and how much of a challenge it's going to be to get there.

JK: Here's one last question. When we started writing this book, I told people that it would find a market with the "board-gaming community." But does that term even make sense? When I go to a gaming convention, and I'm hanging out with folks playing war-games or hardcore Eurogames, there really isn't much interaction between us and the folks in the next room dressed up in costumes and playing highly immersive (and sometimes emotionally expres-sive) role-playing games—except maybe at the water fountain or lunch area. As I argued in my chapter on *Scrabble*, I sometimes feel like the term "board-gaming community" now makes as much sense as "music community." To reformulate a question I asked in that chapter: How much do heavy-metal head-bangers and, say, season-ticket opera-goers have in common?

Gamers are always proselytizing to their friends, trying to get them to try gaming. And one of my hopes was, and remains, that this book would encourage non-gamers to see gaming as a more intellectually rich experience than just rolling dice and collecting cards. I hope this happens. But regardless of whether this effort succeeds, the deep dive into board-gaming sub-subcultures that this book has prompted has left me less optimistic about wider community-building within the board-gaming community—in part because of the explosion of Kickstarter-financed titles in every conceivable genre.

When I was a kid, you *had* to branch out and try new games and genres, because there just weren't that many good games out there. You couldn't afford to be picky. These days, it's different. You like train and rail games? There are literally thousands. Space exploration? Same.

Or maybe I am thinking of this the wrong way. Maybe board games are better thought of as a tool for *other* communities to bond—not as the basis of community itself. As I write this, I see there is an event called "Queer Gayme Night" scheduled for a downtown Toronto café. My first-blush response was "I wonder if I would be allowed to attend (even though I'm a straight cis dude)." Which would have made sense twenty years ago, when it really was hard to find a gaming meet-up. But that's changed. And gaming is now sufficiently mainstream that organizers now can apparently attract a critical mass to a game night even when targeting sub-demographics, such as LGBT gamers, who in turn can use these activities to build up their own communities. I'm hoping that in the future, the same will be true in, say, churches, mosques, synagogues and schools. (I am disappointed to report that none of my kids' schools have active gaming clubs)

JM: I think popular culture in general has gotten niche-ier over the past couple decades. The TV-watching community is no longer so much about a few big TV shows that everyone ends up chatting about while standing near a strange device called a "water cooler." Instead, there's this massive profusion of options, ranging from hugely popular HBO productions to obscure YouTube shows, so everyone can seek out the material that speaks most directly to their own tastes. In some cases, I think this can actually be a bad thing. For example, when it comes to news media, some people simply listen to whoever they already agree with and dismiss all other voices as fake news.

But in most areas, including the realm of games, I think it's largely a good thing, and not just because we're no longer stuck playing the same tired old games all the time. In the world of electronic games, the so-called "Triple-A" big-budget players are getting weaker, producing retreads of the same stale, transparently monetized games they made last year, with few titles anyone can really get excited about. Meanwhile, in the indie game space there's a ton of amazing stuff to discover, much like in the world of tabletop games today.

But even with all that variety and fragmentation among the player base, I think game players do have one significant thing in common with one another, and that is their tendency to ask questions that start with the words "What if?" What if I build my settlement here instead of there? What if the Germans had taken and held Stalingrad in 1943? What if a dragon and a robot teamed up against a vampire? Some people are so focused on the world as it is that they have no interest in thinking about the world as it could be, and those people tend to think of games as a waste of time, because they only exist (or at least they only matter) in our imagination.

I think the differences among different kinds of game players often come down to which "What if" questions we tend to ask. Eurogames, conflict simulations, role-playing games—they all ask different questions, but they all invite players to consider the possibility of creating different worlds that branch off from their decisions, the products of their own free will. Typically, those questions involve things within the imaginary worlds of the games themselves. But over time, they can expand out beyond the tabletop, leading to questions like: What if I could play with other people who are like me? What if I could find deeper connections and feel less like I'm alone in this world?

Maybe even: what if I started a game club at my school? Would we have to play the same kinds of games my dad likes? (Psst! Hey kids, the answer to that last question is no!)

Sometimes I find myself taking my evangelism for play very seriously. The suffering caused by our modern sense of disconnection and loneliness, combined with the power of games to help bring us together, makes the mission feel urgent to me. There's also all the damage caused by our overpowering fear of showing weakness or doing anything that might appear even vaguely like a mistake. Everyone seems so afraid of judgment that they can't ever bring themselves to even think about being truly playful. So much life wasted, so much potential for joy and discovery just lost. So for me, the need to de-stigmatize play has become such a big deal that I can end up feeling really discouraged when it seems like I'm not getting through.

Sometimes that discouragement blinds me from noticing something rather important though: those same people are have already shown their willingness to actually get together in the same little corner of space-time to enjoy each other's company for a while. And if they get used to spending time together, maybe they will become less fearful of the kind of judgment and derision that makes failure so scary, and consequently makes playfulness difficult or impossible for so many people.

So maybe it's good that there are all those various communities are there, playing among various kinds of people. The more time they spend playing together without judgment, playing all their varied genres of games in all their varied play styles, people will find their groups and their games. Maybe the best thing I can do is just to help them find each other and get started. And if I fail, or *when* I fail, I'll just try again.

ACKNOWLEDGEMENTS

I am grateful to Jonathan Kay, who got me started as a professional writer and came up with the idea for this book. I thank Sean Jacquemain for showing what beautiful objects board games can be. I owe thanks to everyone who has ever played a game with me. There isn't room to list them all but particular inspirations and material for the chapters in this book came from Todd Campbell, Mandy Jelsma, Dan Legault, Allie Moser, Andrew Nie, Matthew Migliardi, Dave Schokking, Steve Tassie, and Mark Whiting. For further inspiration as well as much-needed support and advice through it all, my love and my thanks to Liz Garfield, Mike Garfield, Naomi Gurarie, Coco Lee, Michael Moriarity, Scott Emerson Moyle, Wendy Newman, and Lynette Terrill.

Joan Moriatity

Thanks to my co-author Joan for her encouragement and imagination, and to my wife Jennifer Good for allowing me to do so much "research." Also thanks to John and Kristen Chew for serving as both subjects and editors, and to all my regular gaming partners: Michael McNally, the brothers Kalman (Daniel, Josh and David), Wai-Kwong Wong, Andy Beaton, Mark Watson, J.R. Tracy and Phil Willow.

Jonathan Kay